Deadicated to the Afterlife

Louise Hermann

Deadicated to the Afterlife

Copyright © 2010 Louise Hermann
All rights reserved. No part of this publication may be reproduced, stored in a retrieval system or transmitted in any form or by any means, electronic, mechanical, photocopying, recording or otherwise, without the prior written permission of the publisher.

The information, views, opinions and visuals expressed in this publication are solely those of the author(s) and do not reflect those of the publisher. The publisher disclaims any liabilities or responsibilities whatsoever for any damages, libel or liabilities arising directly or indirectly from the contents of this publication.

A copy of this publication can be found in the National Library of Australia.

ISBN: 978-1-921791-80-2 (pbk.)

Published by Book Pal
www.bookpal.com.au

For *Team Spirit*

Acknowledgements

On this side of life

To all of my family, friends, helpers and supporters for believing and trusting in my work.

A special thank you to all of those who allowed me to share their story for the greater healing purpose of humanity.

Gratitude to my own soul for taking on this remarkable journey in this life.

On the other side

To all my deceased relatives and friends who are a constant beacon of guiding light.

A special acknowledgement of my spirit guides, friends and helpers who are known to me as *Team Spirit* and an inspiration to many souls.

I would also like to acknowledge my editor Sabina Collins for her patience and dedication. A special thank you to the proofreaders as well.

Only a few names have been changed in this book.

For more information on Louise, please visit *www.louisehermann.com*

Contents

Chapter 1
Small to Medium 1

Chapter 2
To Make God Laugh, Tell Him Your Plans 12

Chapter 3
The Catholics and the Medium 24

Chapter 4
The Apprenticeship 38

Chapter 5
Mechanics of Mediumship 50

Chapter 6
Bridging Two Worlds as One 64

Chapter 7
There is No Death 78

Chapter 8
Healing Hands 89

Chapter 9
When Your Time is Up 104

Chapter 10
High-flying Fiona 117

Chapter 11
    Knowing Me, Knowing You 128

Chapter 12
    The Myths of Murders and Suicides 139

Chapter 13
    Neither Here Nor There 155

Chapter 14
    Chook 171

Chapter 15
    Children and Animal Spirits 180

Chapter 16
    Can Spirit Predict? 196

Chapter 17
    Everything is Borrowed 209

Chapter 18
    Peace Among the Deceased 219

Chapter 19
    Journeys to the Other Side 232

Chapter 20
    Signals and Signposts 251

Chapter 21
    Team Spirit Speaks 265

Chapter 1

Small to Medium

You can never grow if you are not willing to extend yourselves.
Team Spirit

The train station had a clear and distinctive long concrete platform and there I could see a young boy and a woman slipping off this platform onto the railway tracks. I reached out to help them but there was nothing I could do. They tumbled straight onto the tracks and my little arms couldn't grab them. As I strained to help them, they were gone. All that was left behind were my arms in the air as I woke up from this recurring dream. It wasn't until one morning a few weeks later that I thought how strange it was that my dream was on the television news and that other people could see it as well. I thought perhaps others could try and save them, too, and not just me every morning in my dreams. Obviously that was not to be. At such a young age, I had no understanding of what predictions were and that people actually died.

People ask me: *"What was the first mediumistic experience you had and when?"* Looking back, there were so many at a very young age it would be impossible to record them all. From the age of around three onwards, spirit people often called me and I remember making our meeting place under the house. Coming from a large family there was no personal space at all, so I can now see why we chose to meet there. I can still smell the damp dirt under the house as I crawled and made my way under. We would just sit there together and they would give me a knowingness about certain things that I seemed to naturally understand.

I grew up one of eight children and a twin to my sister, Therese. I have since met two other brothers from my father's first marriage, so I'm now one of 10 children. I was the elder twin born in Tamworth, NSW, Australia, on October 21, 1973. Therese managed to go home with the family and I, the physically weaker one, stayed behind in hospital for a couple of months on feeding tubes. Therese and I were opposite in looks. As a child, I had short blonde curly hair and Therese had straight black hair. I have a distinctive little red birthmark on the back of my neck where I'm sure Therese's impatience pushed me out into this world. Even though we differ in looks, we are similar in personality in many ways.

Therese was no doubt the more protective twin and I strongly believe she was sent to me in this life as a living guide. People often ask if she shares my gift. I believe she does but in many other ways. She may not stand on a platform and directly demonstrate to audiences that their loved ones are present from the spirit world, however she is highly intuitive and carries a level of wisdom and strength that I see as similar to my spirit guides from the other side. Mediumship involves assistance from both sides of the veil and Therese has been a major player in the delivery of the work of spirit into the physical world.

There was never a sense of loneliness in my childhood. We were all, and still are, a very close-knit family who love and care for one another on a much deeper level than most. We have a natural understanding of people's needs and we are all very giving in personality. I'm proud to admit that I did not come from a family of material wealth, but instead one of wealth in understanding and compassion for others. The family unit I was born into couldn't have been better chosen for the path of work that lay ahead for me.

My mother, Barbara, is a very compassionate and giving person with a remarkable faith that all in life will be well and a greater plan is at hand for all. Her strength of raising eight children with such high morals and honest values, both within us and towards others, is an accomplishment any mother may hope to achieve. Despite our family having restrictions on the financial side of life, she always dressed us well and presented us with a confidence that anything in life could be obtained through hard work.

My mother is a great believer in the spirit world and she would often serve her time in the spiritualist church. I have clear memories of her attending services on a Sunday and had no idea that one day I, too, would be serving spirit on a platform to audiences. Throughout my own journey with the spirit world, Mum never intervened. Her comment to me was simply, *"If this is your path, they will teach you everything."* And so from a young age I just listened to the spirit people, who showed me all different ways of life, from both sides of the veil, without questioning too much of it.

In a clear vision one day, the spirit world showed me the importance of choosing my parents for the work I was to take part in. In this vision, they showed Mum in the 1960s, years before I was born, in a little mini skirt, dancing and enjoying her time with my father. On a few occasions when I had visitations to the other side through out-of-body experiences, they also showed me the importance of energy in my chosen name.

There were three main reasons why the name *Louise Hermann* was chosen. Firstly, the name Louise had the letter "u" (You) before the letter "i" (I), which is a major part of my teaching to others: "Think not just of oneself but of others as well." Secondly, the name Louise represents the closest in letters to my greatest teaching: "Love is". My surname of Hermann represents a balance of female energy (Her) and male energy (Man). An additional letter "n" was placed on my surname to give greater strength to the male energy side of me since I was born female. When I returned from my spirit world journey, I found this information to be quite fascinating and now believe there is a higher energetic importance in all names given to everyone.

My mother has always been a very attractive lady, just under six feet in height with long legs, dark hair and magical blue eyes. She was a natural ballroom dancer and kept on dancing right up until the birth of her youngest child, little Barbara. She never dieted or spoke of such things and kept her wonderful figure through natural genetics and everyday hard work. Her mind and body did not show the toughness that life had handed her at a young age. She lost her own mother at 12 years of age.

Growing up, I always remember Mum's trusting belief in the greater spirit and the power of the Divine. I will never forget the immense faith my mother had on a day when a veterinary told both Therese and I that Blacky, our horse, would not survive a serious dose of colic. We were all standing underneath a large tree in the front yard when Mum placed her hand on his forehead and closed her eyes with great intensity. She turned to the vet and said, *"Yes he will,"* and then named another vet who would help. Therese and I quickly tracked down the new vet and within five days of nursing Blacky in the backyard under the instructions of the new vet, he did indeed survive. That was more than 20 years ago and Blacky is alive and well and still under the care of the vet chosen by Mum.

My father, Kurt, on the other hand, played a greater part in my life in other ways. He was a migrant from Germany and during the Second World War he had seen and witnessed many things a young child should not have been exposed to. He never speaks of the war but on the rare occasion he does, he tells of the Jewish families they fed and the fear of being caught for doing so. As a young boy, Dad reached starvation levels while captured and was forced to leave behind his mother who was deteriorating fast through weight loss from typhoid. His mother had previously survived a line-up shooting by a Russian soldier. Now it seemed her life would definitely fade away. However, within six months of minimal treatment this remarkable woman not only survived the war but became the most influential woman in my life. I will discuss Grandma in further detail later.

I was around eight years of age when the feeling of never being lonely changed for a little while and an overwhelming sense of sadness and abandonment overcame me. I can clearly recall that morning waking after a visitation to the other side knowing that my friends would not be returning to the earth plane. There was to be a changing of the guards (or is that the guides) and it would take some time for me to understand what this was all about. I can clearly remember explaining to Therese the deep sadness of my spirit friends no longer returning. I was so sad I even told the other kids in the class all about it – that the little people were not coming back. I just wanted to go and visit them once more or have them visit me. Unfortunately, this was not to be the case – the spirit world had greater plans ahead for me.

I was raised in Newcastle, Australia, for most of my life. When I was around nine years of age, my family moved to another house and this house had a presence about it that I had never experienced before. Immediately after we moved in, there was a lot of spirit activity which fascinated me on all levels – and my siblings as well. It was no longer just meeting spirits under the house, this time we had a regular visitor and she was coming directly to me. An older lady in a tartan style dress stood clearly near my bed and we chatted for hours. I was on the bottom of a red double bunk and Therese was at the top. I loved the fact that the lady stood behind the ladder but I could see all of her – no body parts were missing or blocked from my vision. She was my new friend and after a few weeks, I realised she must have been different because she wore the same clothing every night and didn't smell.

After a while, I explained to Mum that this lady was visiting and chatting all night. I described her in detail and provided a name and Mum said she would investigate further. The neighbours confirmed that she had indeed passed away in the house some years earlier and always wore the dress I described when she was gardening. As a medium, confirmation is of importance but at such a young age it didn't seem to matter at all. The visitations from the old lady lasted some months of nightly chatter until eventually she no longer visited. It wasn't long after this that the intensity and type of visitations would change and they would be from someone I least expected.

It was 1984 and I was only a kid, a 10-year-old child with no idea really of how everything operated at a much higher level. There was a knock at the door very late at night from the police. My eldest brother Andrew, who was 20 years of age, had been reported missing and feared drowned a couple of hours before. I couldn't understand how a tall, six foot five young man could be harmed by anyone or anything. He was in the navy cadets as a young teenager, so how could he have possibly drowned? He was strong. He used to lift me up to the ceiling when I enjoyed the rush of seeing the floor from so high. He also picked us up from school on the back of his motorbike just for the thrill of the short ride home a couple of streets away. Perhaps they got it wrong, perhaps incorrect information was sent to the police. To me it was not possible but to my elder brothers and sisters as I heard them screaming, it seemed quite possible and real. My sister Tanya had experienced strong feelings earlier that evening that Andrew was cold and needed his blankets.

The hours turned into days and there was no sign of Andrew. My clear last memories of my brother are of him sitting on his motorbike at the front of our house at dawn as he got ready for his big adventure. He was travelling to the Northern Territory with a friend for a trip that would last for months. He had his life ahead of him and his last postcard – sent a couple of days before he went missing – indicated that he was having the adventure of a lifetime. I clearly remember picking a four-leaf clover at school the week before, knowing that a big sign was to come. Something would change but I had no idea what it would be.

As the days passed, I watched the neighbours come together and support my parents. My father and my brother, Mark, made their way to the Northern Territory. I can't recall any support from other kids, instead only the cruelty children can place on others during such a testing time. Andrew was in the Northern Territory which was known as a crocodile area. In the days he was missing, I remember kids coming up to me and saying that a crocodile had taken him and we would never find him. This torment was unnecessary for a child who was trying to come to terms with a missing brother – let alone the possibility of such further horror occurring.

It was confirmed some days later that Andrew had indeed passed away and his body was on its way home. He had drowned in a swimming hole where there was a sudden drop in temperature and a dangerous underlying current. This was far from the stories told by the kids but it didn't make the grief any easier. I had lost my eldest brother, someone who I thought was invincible and he wasn't coming back. My brothers had an empty bed in their room and I just waited for Andrew to turn up out of the blue and say it was all a joke. He was a joker all right. He played plenty of tricks on us all the time – but I somehow knew it was not the case in this instance.

Shandy was Andrew's dog – a fluffy, orange-looking wire-haired stray with attitude. I haven't seen a dog like her since and perhaps never will. She was strange in looks and personality but Andrew loved her to bits. He spent most of his teenage years pulling out and rebuilding car engines and Shandy was alongside him everywhere he went. Around three weeks after his passing, I clearly remember her slowly refusing to eat and within days she just lay down on the front porch and passed away. I know she waited for him to come home and I know she willed her way to the other side. Andrew was her life and so she simply decided to follow him. In a strange sort of way it gave me comfort that he would not be alone in the spirit world – he would now have his special friend with him.

My parents did the best they could do to keep us all together and to bring as much normality into our lives as possible. Andrew's passing taught me a lot about grief and the vast differences of understanding between adults and children. Four months after

Andrew passed, our parents bought us a pool for Christmas. I remember the look on the kids' faces. Why would they buy us a pool when Andrew had just drowned? Looking back, my parents had been through a lot as children themselves, facing death at a very young age. I know they didn't want us to fear the water and they were right – today we spend most of our leisure time together as brothers and sisters on the beach.

A few months after Andrew's passing, I heard my named being called in the middle of the night telling me to go to the hallway. I have clear memories of getting into trouble as a child for cutting a hole in the hallway carpet to play marbles. The younger children, including me, were obsessed with marbles and coming from a large family there were plenty of players to compete with. In the middle of the night as I heard my named being called, I remember Andrew smiling at the end of the hallway and laughing about the marbles. The hallway seemed much longer when he was standing in it. It was now full of light and an overwhelming sense of protection came from him. He had not gone anywhere at all – he was back and he seemed to have that smiling, joking face again. His funeral was just some sort of party and he had validated to me the greatest teaching of the spirit world and mediumship: *"There is no death."*

Chapter 2

To Make God Laugh, Tell Him Your Plans

A single soul in tune with the vibration of many souls can be more powerful than many souls singing their own tune.
Team Spirit

There's an old saying: *"To make God laugh, tell him your plans."* There is so much truth in this statement. People ask me who God is and whether there's a greater plan for our lives. I have no doubt there is a greater plan and you'll see so much of this throughout the book. In terms of God – well, that would be impossible for me to interpret as I believe the answer is far greater than the human mind can ever comprehend. The closest I have personally come to the interpretation of this is when I have been momentarily hit with so much light throughout my body that I am connected to everything and everyone all at once in the universe. No words can express the love I feel in those moments and I believe that many people experience these emotions upon physical death.

I do not personally use the word God on a day-to-day basis. My preference of words is the Divine or

Universal Force as I do not believe there is one energy in the sky directing people's lives. Also, too much death has occurred in vain over this one word, so I like to use a more general term that doesn't categorise religion. At the end of a reading, I often hear the spirits say to me, "*God Bless You*," and I know they understand this force while in spirit. The universe has a level of intelligence far greater than that of man and I believe that all free will and choices are executed in such a divine order as part of this greater plan.

Looking back throughout my younger years, I can now clearly see this greater plan for my own life unfolding. Shortly after the death of my brother, I spent my time hanging out in the afternoons with my little friend, Trevor. I remember his parents giving him 40 cents every day and he always wanted to share half with me. He was a kind soul who always took the time to wait for me after school and we used to chat about everything. Of course, when you're 11 years of age, a boyfriend is just a male friend who shares common interests with you. There was nothing physical in our relationship. We were just kids.

It was not until some years later, at a school reunion, that I realised what Trevor had taught me. We had both drifted along through our lives, as kids do. Later on, in his twenties, Trevor took his own life. It was soon after this that I received a visitation from another boy in spirit, Rodney, who I had spent a lot of time with as a child. He had also taken his life. I decided to visit Rodney's family and deliver a message from him after his spirit visited me.

As I sat in the park around the corner from Rodney's house and delivered the message to his sister, I could see myself as a child playing with both these boys on the swings. What were the odds that two of my close male friends, who didn't even know one another, had taken their own lives? I hadn't seen them in many years but it still affected me greatly. I immediately received a response from the spirit world that there was a part of me at that young age that could already read that their energetic choices were heading in that direction. It was this empathetic part of me that tried to help them and to lead them in a direction of a more positive free will and choice. Obviously it was not to be but their lives impacted me in such a manner that their teaching would heal many others along the path of my mediumship life.

Most of my teenage years were pretty normal – well as normal as they could be. I continued to have regular visitations from the spirit world and many out-of-body experiences. There was a time in my life when I could clearly recall panicking when I couldn't make my way back into the physical body quickly enough on my return from the spirit world. An overwhelming sense of calmness would be placed over me, however the conscious side of my mind was too impatient. I would always view my body on the bed and it felt like I was coming out of anaesthesia when reconnecting. Over time this panic was something I learnt to manage and even today I become all too aware of what's occurring upon landing. Now I have a little technique I use when I feel like I'm being pulled from my body. I place my right knee at a certain angle and it becomes a focus point when I'm reconnecting with the physical body.

For me, takeoff from the body is a much more pleasurable experience than landing, as some energetic adjustments need to be made to my energy field when drawing close to the earth plane again. Over the years, these experiences have given me a greater level of understanding of the difficulties our loved ones must encounter when they draw close to the physical world in order to blend themselves with the energy field of the medium. It makes sense why a spirit who has blended with a medium before can come back a second time through another medium and seem to understand the mechanics much better. Many spirits have told me this and some even consider themselves "experts" – that makes me laugh!

After high school, I moved onto university and completed an honours degree, specialising in economics. Once I graduated, I worked at the university in a management role and I had no idea how to use a computer. I would often say to the staff, *"Ask and you will receive,"* with the strong belief that everything is provided by the universe. With no prior experience in computer engineering, I started to develop a database called "Louise", where all the administrative dreams could come true. I asked the staff to write on a large roll of butcher paper what they would like in an ideal working environment. Throughout my life I have never been short of enthusiasm and looking back it must have been overwhelming for them when "Hurricane Hermann" arrived to manage their working unit.

With no formal training or assistance, over a few months the skeleton of "Louise" was created. Day by day I added the flesh and soon she was completed, with many functions we were all very pleased with. I worked on the database in the office on my own after work every night and I believe this was the training for my inspirational channelling work for the spirit world. The initial inspiration and guidance came from both spirit and me and it was not until years later that I saw the greater importance of that initial project. Soon, our working unit at the university won an award for the new computer system and I was off to Canberra, the capital of Australia, to build a similar computer system for another university. Then, I left the university and moved to Sydney to commence work with a global software company on a career path as a computer engineer. I worked for some years as a technical development consultant building software for large organisations.

If someone had told me years before this would be the greater plan for me when I commenced university studies, I'd most definitely have laughed. I didn't even like computers – I had no interest in them at all. Obviously there were other players at hand and on the first evening of my arrival in Sydney a distinctive visitation from the spirit world would confirm this further.

It was September 4, 2000, when I arrived in Sydney. The Olympic Games were commencing and there was an atmosphere of excitement everywhere. I had the opportunity to stay in a house where police officers lived. This would be a temporary residence until I settled in Sydney and found my own place. I was taken to a damp, dark room at the front of the house where I slept on a mattress on the floor for a few weeks.

On the first few nights, there was an overwhelming sense of being in someone else's space and that I definitely did not belong in that bedroom. Soon the spirit of a young boy manifested himself next to my mattress. He sat near my head on the floor, with his legs crossed and was as clear and solid as a child in physical form. I ran out to the lounge room and asked if anyone knew this young spirit boy in my room. They explained that he had lost his life at the front of the house some time ago and the details I described were very accurate. This first outburst to a group of rational and sceptical people who required evidence would be the beginning of sharing my spiritual experiences to the public at large.

In these earlier years in Sydney, I found myself living and working with rationally minded people. I lived with police officers who required evidence on most matters and my fellow employees in the computer software company were also very logical in nature. My balance between the left-brain logic and the right-brain intuitive and creative side would bring about my investigative side. I would need to provide evidence to the recipients of the spirit messages that there is life after death and that their loved ones did indeed survive the physical death process.

I clearly recall the last conversation I had with my 94-year-old grandmother, who lived in Germany. She had survived World War II and was blind and she had a knowingness about most things in life. At the time of my brother's passing she was in Israel and had a distinctive visitation in a dream of an Aboriginal lady, who told her to call Australia immediately. Once she called, her fears were confirmed that my brother was indeed missing and later confirmed drowned.

One evening, Grandma said to me that things didn't feel right with her. The last time I spoke to her, she told me she felt that her time on earth was coming to an end and my father should come to Germany immediately. She wasn't unwell at the time of the phone call. She lived at home in her unit rather than a home for the elderly, however, soon after the call she had deteriorated and was in hospital. My father caught a flight to Germany and a few days after his arrival she peacefully passed over into the spirit world. At the exact time of her passing, I was booking flights to leave Australia for Germany. In that moment I felt that someone had taken my heart away.

Grandma (Anneliese) was the most influential woman in my life. I would often visit her in Germany and she taught me so much about myself and life in general. I can't help but laugh right now – she always said that one day a book would be written with her life in it. She was an absolutely beautiful woman, inside and out. In her early years, she was tall, blonde, had olive skin and beautiful big eyes. Raising my father during the war was hard. Grandma was a single divorced mother and she always held her head high throughout her tough life. After surviving the war and a serious bout of typhoid, she began to rebuild her life, starting with nothing. She was soon financially secure again by working as an assistant for some of Germany's finest architects. As a result of her illness during the war, she became blind in her mid-fifties and this ended her career.

Every opportunity Grandma had, she visited our family in Australia for months at a time. She would take us to the beach, which seemed impossible since she couldn't see. We all listened to her and in the early days we taught her better English and she taught us German. Over the years, Grandma perfected English and the children created a half-

English, half-German language, like most families with multicultural backgrounds do. I'll never forget the smell of her little leather purse as she handed us money. We had to count it out loud and purchase the best bargain lunch we could with our budget. She instilled in us all at a young age that we needed to work for everything and that anything was possible through hard work.

When we were children, it was not unusual to lie near Grandma in bed and have an afternoon sleep with her as she stroked our hair. She had the softest brown hands and loved her grandchildren more than any Grandma I knew. We had the coolest Grandma, who spent all her time not only with us but also with our cats, dogs, birds, horses and regular friends. She cut down to the basics on most things in life to assist my parents financially in raising their eight children.

For Grandma, assisting was not a chore. She had grandchildren and when help was required she always stepped in with unconditional love. Every time I go to the post office I think of Grandma. I'm still amazed at how a blind lady in Germany bought clothing and toys, carried them to the post office and sent the large packages to Australia. The gratitude I have for her in my life is immense and I have been blessed to have such a soul to call my grandma.

As soon as Grandma passed into the spirit world, I could feel her presence immediately. It was 7.30pm Australian time and I spent the whole night on my own in tears. It was the longest night of my life as I cried myself in and out of sleep while reading the letters we had written to one another. The strongest woman I had ever known was now physically gone and I would never be able to speak and laugh with her on the phone again. Even as a medium, there is a part of the human side of us that wonders how such strong people leave the earth plane.

The day after Grandma's passing, my sisters travelled from Newcastle to Sydney to drive me to the airport. I was so sad that I couldn't even speak to the travel agent when I purchased my plane tickets. My heart was truly broken because I didn't get the chance to say goodbye to our Grandma-ma. I said my goodbyes to my sisters and boarded the plane. Before I knew it, I was on a long journey from Australia to Germany. The last place any grieving person wants to be is on a plane full of hundreds of people who are mostly excited about a new holiday, or arriving home after completing one.

This long journey on my own was a time of deep reflection on what life was all about and how quickly it can be taken from us. It reminded me of a male colleague who, not long before, had received news whilst in America that his son had been killed in an accident in Australia. I wondered how terrible this must have been for him, taking that long flight home on his own.

I caught my connecting flight to Frankfurt and then boarded a train from Cologne to Aachen. I'd had hardly any sleep and the train journey brought back so many memories for me. I remembered the excitement of the first trip on my own to Germany and how Grandma and Aunt Kate (Grandma's sister) met me at Cologne train station. Together the three of us caught a train to Aachen and laughed all the way to their place. Over the next two months we spent quality time together, sharing a beautiful white Christmas in Austria. These fond memories, as I reached Aachen train station, were far from the emotions I was feeling right now. Within 10 minutes, I found Aunt Kate sitting in the park, lost and alone. Her sister of over 90 years was now in the spirit world.

I could see the pain on my father's face when I arrived at Grandma's place. The smell of her unit was so real and the Australian souvenirs on the wall reminded me of home. As I took a bath in her tub, everything seemed to become a lot clearer. Nothing had separated us at all, not even the distance across the world. Why would physical death be any different? Grandma was simply on a new journey and one day we would reunite together in spirit form.

Over the next few days, my Dad's girlfriend Helga (now my stepmother) arrived in Germany. I watched Dad age quickly as he organised Grandma's remains to be sent back to Australia. It took me back to my childhood when Dad travelled a distance to bring back my brother's physical body. Upon viewing Grandma, the funeral director was full of praise about how great she looked but when I arrived, I could not feel her presence in the room. Her lifeless body was simply a heavy coat to me that had been removed from her spirit. She was now carefree and her body was just a reminder that she had once lived a physical existence here on earth.

While spending a few weeks with Aunt Kate, I documented Grandma's life in a little booklet that would become an important part of her funeral service. Her ashes were to be later scattered on a beach in Australia, which was the place where she felt most at home. Before I knew it, I was on my way home from Germany on a direct flight to Sydney. I was tired from the few weeks away and, miraculously, the seats next to me had been cancelled so I could lie across them and go to sleep. While in a deep sleep state travelling home, I was to have a premonition that would alter the path of my mediumship life forever.

Chapter 3

The Catholics and the Medium

Picture yourself in a scene of doubt and your views will have rocky mountains and troubled waters.
Team Spirit

As the plane arrived at Sydney airport with the beautiful sunrise reflecting on the water, I still had a level of anxiety about arriving home. The previous two weeks had been traumatic, organising the shipping of Grandma's belongings and her remains back to Australia and now I had a clear vision of my laptop computer being stolen at work. I made my way to the office and my laptop was absolutely fine and secure. I shared my premonition with a few work colleagues and left it at that. Perhaps I was overtired and stressed from the long journey and too much imagination had come into play.

The next day, after a good night's sleep, I arrived at the office to discover that not only had my laptop been stolen but that a number of others were gone as well. I remember everyone looking at me and before long an investigator arrived at work. The investigation wasn't focused on me, however I found myself answering questions with information I had already provided to my colleagues before the theft. The investigator was a little suspicious, given the fact that I mentioned to him that certain cameras on certain levels were not working, plus a possible scenario of how the suspect could have escaped quite easily. To me it was obvious how they did it. Not long after that, the investigators stopped asking me questions and the topic was dropped. I've often wondered what they did with the information but at the time I was just pleased that they stopped bothering me.

Now that I had openly shared a premonition with a group of work colleagues, with evidence, it was time for the spirit world to accelerate their work. I had regular visitations from the spirits throughout the night providing messages for people with whom I worked. At the time, I was a technical computer engineer with responsibilities across 16 countries, so the range of visitations was vast across many continents. The rational part of me began to ask the spirits for some evidence of their identification and "proof of consciousness", a term I use to describe information given by the spirits on observation of their loved ones after physical death. This proves that their consciousness, or personality, has survived physical death and they are well aware of what their loved ones are doing here on the earth plane by providing me with this evidence.

Looking back at those early days of sharing mediumship with my work colleagues, I see the determination and stamina required for spirit communication. The spirit world once said to me that they were important factors in the delivery of their work. The ability to put your own ego aside and simply serve the spirit world would be difficult for most people. They would fear losing their jobs, being judged or seen as plain crazy. Either way I didn't care – I just did what I did without hesitation or thinking about it too much. The spirits were real to me and I had the gift to bring their personalities back to life and provide healing for those who were left behind grieving on the earth plane.

Perhaps one of the most difficult tests the spirit world can give a medium is to have them deliver a message not only to their Human Resources Manager, who pays them but also their boss. Kathleen was in charge of managing our division from a human resources perspective. Her deceased grandmother came to tell me that Kathleen was expecting a little girl. She shared other very personal details which I couldn't possibly have known and without hesitation I arranged a meeting with Kathleen at lunch that day. She wondered why we had to meet that particular day and when I shared the news with her she was completely shocked.

Kathleen had not shared her pregnancy news with anyone and her grandmother gave her some additional action items to be executed that evening with relatives on this side of life. I had no idea how Kathleen would process it all but shortly afterwards I received a lovely thank you email confirming that the message was accepted with gratitude. Even today, some years later, when I see her daughter in the office, I smile at the gift her grandmother brought that day.

The delivery of a message to my boss seemed much more difficult. Angela was a high-flying achiever who had done very well for herself at such a young age. At the time, she was managing quality assurance for software products across 16 countries and she worked very long hours to achieve her goals. When we did spend time together we always discussed work and the next level of work ahead of us. There was never any personal time for chatter and so I was really surprised when her grandmother was next off the ranks from the spirit world.

Angela's grandmother visited a number of times before I had the courage to deliver the message. I asked my guides on the other side to give me a prompt, a reason to start the discussion with her. One morning, Angela called me into the office and asked if I wanted to take on the extra responsibility of a larger role at work. I explained to her that I had extracurricular activities of a high priority that required me to always leave work on time. Her face quickly changed when I explained to her that I communicated with those who had passed over, *"and by the way, your grandmother has been visiting, too"*.

Soon, I was writing on her whiteboard providing evidence of the visitation and explaining how it all worked between the two worlds, including the varying vibrational frequencies. After a short time, Angela packed up and left the office early. This was out of character for her, so I was left wondering how she had taken all this information in.

That evening, I clearly remember lying across my bed and thinking:"*oh well, perhaps today was my last day at work*". But Angela's grandmother arrived again in spirit that night and placed a beautiful bunch of flowers on my chest with her spirit aura shining with colours I'd never seen before. She was excited and a boost of confidence beamed throughout my body. I knew in that instant that everything would be fine. Angela would see the evidence and know that I meant no harm but simply wanted to provide a message of love from her grandmother.

The next day when Angela arrived in the office, she said she'd done some research. People like me were called "mediums" and she gladly accepted the message from her grandmother based on the evidence that was given. Angela had been brought up as a Catholic, so the initial response from her was at a level of uncertainty and unknowingness regarding spiritual realms. Today, Angela and I share many discussions about the spirit world and since that day our conversations have been more personal and no longer just about work. She loves to attend my mediumship events and really does take on board the spiritual teachings of the other side. I have no doubt she was guided to me as part of the greater plan, to allow me to work for the spirit world and also continue my career. Without her support, it would have been much more difficult for me to balance the two worlds and those I report to on both sides of life.

Soon after the incident with Angela, I was woken by a young female spirit from India. She explained to me that she had passed as a result of an accident and that I needed to deliver a message to a man who would be arriving at the Sydney office the following Monday. I documented the evidence and waited for Monday to arrive. Early that morning, a tall young man arrived from India and was introduced to me. I decided to hold no further discussions with him until after work hours so my evidence would remain strong when I approached him and I wouldn't be mixing my work time with spirit time.

Later that evening, I knocked on his office door and sat down after he invited me in. I didn't waste any time – I began to draw on the whiteboard. I drew the front door of his sister's house in India, as well as the house plans, current renovations and family structure. I then went on to describe the day she passed and how it could easily have been him that day and not her. He was about to get married and she asked me to tell him to stop feeling guilty and to move on with his life. It was her time and not his and she was the one who was meant to pass into the spirit world that day.

She asked him to take a specific personal object to his wedding day and she would be there waiting for him. The young man burst into tears when I delivered the message and quickly asked if he could call his family in India to deliver the healing news. It was one of the most emotionally relieving messages I had given to date. He had been so traumatised by his sister's death a few years earlier that it had left him with deep levels of depression and guilt. This message from the spirit world was soon to create another turn in my mediumship pathway.

Around three weeks after the visitation of the Indian lady, I was invited to go to India for work to train a large group of colleagues. I was excited as I had travelled to many countries around the world but this would be my first visit to India. The spirit world informed me that a close work colleague in another office, Zita, would be visiting India at the same time. I called her and it seemed our schedules were almost identical, so we decided to have a stopover for four days in Singapore for some relaxation before a few weeks of hard work.

Before we left for India, Zita and I arranged to go to the Indian consulate in Sydney to obtain work visas. As we travelled together by train, I noticed a very large ball of dark energy coming towards me from the station near the consulate. I had no idea what it was so I just documented it in my diary and briefly shared it with Zita. She didn't make any further comments since she could not see what I saw, so I dropped the topic of discussion.

Upon boarding our flight to Singapore, I began to obsess over time. I never wear a watch, so it was strange that I started to notice when time seemed to freeze in my mind. I wrote down the series of times. Once again, I shared this with Zita and she had no idea what I was talking about. Zita was raised a Catholic, a firm believer in the ideology of Catholicism, so such comments of the unseen realms didn't go down very well. Despite our differences, we were very good friends and never at any time attempted to convert one another. We found in the few discussions we had on the subject of spirituality that faith, love and light were common in most belief systems. The only differences were in the delivery of the messages.

When we arrived at the hotel in Singapore, Zita and I were lucky enough to be the 500th customer of the year and were upgraded to the penthouse suite. I was pretty excited but the expression on Zita's face when she discovered that our rooms would be merged into one apartment was priceless. There was no way she was going to sleep in the same room as a medium who had the dead visiting at night. I attempted to encourage her but her decision was final. After check-in, I visited Zita's apartment. She had her rosary beads out near the bed, which was a sure sign that spirits wouldn't be coming anywhere near her throughout the trip.

Over the next few days, Zita and I met up with another work colleague, Shannon. The three of us enjoyed time together, seeing the sights and sampling the fine food of Singapore. Throughout those days, my clairvoyant vision was changing and I would see a large bolt of light and matrix of colours quite often in my vision. One afternoon, I could clearly hear through a tunnel and heard the words "ramble scramble". I continued to document the timings I was receiving and shared them with Zita, even though it made no sense to either of us at the time.

After four days of fun and excitement in Singapore, Zita and I boarded separate flights to India. I was heading to Bangalore and Zita to Hyderabad to work for the next two weeks. Shannon would meet up with us again in Bangalore a couple of weeks later for some more adventures. When I arrived at Bangalore Airport just before midnight, I was sad to see so many people begging for money. It was terrible trying to get my luggage amongst the chaos of the small airport and I was lucky enough for the driver to spot me and get me through the crowd to the car. It wouldn't have been too difficult for him to find me – I'm almost six feet tall with blonde hair, so I stood out in India.

As he drove me to the hotel in Bangalore, it somehow reminded me strongly of Baghdad. I didn't know why but I felt an overwhelming sense of insecurity and the quietness of the long dirt road trip after midnight gave me an untrusting feeling I normally don't get. Once I arrived at the hotel, I checked in and got as much sleep as I could before going to the office the next day.

I remember meeting some guys from NASA downstairs at breakfast and having some interesting conversations about space. The driver picked me up and we began the long trip to the office. I found myself sitting on the edge of my seat the whole way. Not only did I have a mad driver, everyone else on the road was just as crazy. There were so many near misses and potential accidents along the way. I had flashes of the Indian spirit lady and could easily see how these accidents could occur.

Once at work, I was introduced to a senior manager of the company. He welcomed me into his office and began talking about the importance of how people are sent from God to heal others. These people, he said, should be shown the temples of India as part of their gratitude. I just thought it was part of the general talk when you arrived in India, until he personally thanked me for the healing I had provided to the young man who had visited the Sydney office. He said the man was like a son to him and the passing of his sister had left so much guilt in his life. The message from the spirit world had provided him with immense healing and it touched his heart that such peace could arrive from God.

About a week later, I was woken from my sleep at around 2am by a man in spirit who had an amazing presence I had never felt before. He was dressed in an old robe with a distinctive hood that covered his head. He stood clearly to the left of my bed and asked me what I could see on the wall. I said I could only see a butterfly in front of me and he asked me to look further and beyond normal appearances. I then said I could see wood, fire, water and the wind blowing on the beach. He explained the importance of the earth's elements and that there was a path of work I must follow in this life.

He said my teachings were of importance and that my journey to India was to heal many souls passing over into the spirit world. Intrigued by the man who had an overwhelming presence but appearance of simplicity, I asked him who he was. At that moment, he raised his hood and pierced my heart with so much love through his green eyes. I was speechless and full of emotion when he replied that his name was Joseph, the father of Jesus. After he left, I sat on the bed with tears rolling down my face and my heart complete with love. It wasn't who this man was but rather the love he expressed to me that I will never forget.

The next morning, I contacted Zita and told her that Joseph had turned up in my room. Now this one really topped all the stories and her response was almost mute. I knew what Zita was thinking: why would Joseph visit a non-Catholic medium who works with the spirit world. Some hours later, broadcasts across India reported that seven train bombings in Mumbai had just occurred and hundreds of people had lost their lives.

The blackness in the train station when we were getting our visas in Sydney, the "ramble scramble" I heard and the noises of the tunnel were now coming to life. My documented timings coincided with the timings of the train bombings. Many souls had passed into the spirit world through very tragic circumstances. Joseph was correct – so much light was needed to assist these souls to the other side.

Divine intervention to prevent such events could not occur as all souls are given the birthright of free will and choice here on earth. All the divine could do was to assist in healing those who were involved in the events. The shock across India for the next week or so was immense and I just worked my way through it all like any medium does.

After around 10 days in India, Zita and I decided to visit some temples. Permission was given by the tourist guides at the temple to use a camera. I took a photo inside the temple and immediately felt a pull of energy. To my surprise, I had clearly captured the face of a lady on camera. This face didn't have a body. It had clear distinctive features and was sitting on the right side of a statue that represented a goddess.

I quickly showed Zita the photo and she was just as surprised as me. Our experience together with the premonitions, Joseph and train bombings had now opened her mind to new possibilities regarding the spiritual realms. I have no idea about religion in India, so when I explained the temple incident to my work colleagues back in Sydney, with an email of the photo, they advised me to keep it strictly confidential. A picture of this kind in India would be the equivalent of someone capturing a religious figure on camera in the western world. It proved to me that the spirit world has many messengers for different belief systems and religions that ultimately all serve the same purpose of assisting humanity through love and light.

After our short but intense two weeks in India, Zita and I flew back to Sydney with memories we'll never forget. On the flight, I looked out the window and said to Zita, *"There'll be a tsunami in Java very soon."* She laughed and thought here we go again… Within a few hours that was exactly what happened.

Zita, of all the people I know, has had her fair share of proof from the spirit world in a short period of time. We often laugh about it all now, as she has managed to successfully blend her Catholic faith with the teachings of the spirit world. Zita has attended my mediumship events and our friendship has continued to blossom throughout the years.

A lot of my supporters in the public arena come from Catholic backgrounds and I know these earlier tests were given to me from the spirit world to show me how to assist in removing the fears of the afterlife and the work of the spirit world. We are all spiritual beings here for a physical experience and no beliefs, no matter what they are, will ever change this common knowingness amongst all of humanity.

Chapter 4

The Apprenticeship

A key is not required to unlock your potential, simply give your soul permission to open the door.
Team Spirit

The previous time I flew back to Sydney was from Germany and I'd spent the flight thinking of my Grandma and the meaning of life. This time, returning from India, there wasn't much difference. I hadn't personally lost a family member but had experienced the emotions of grief for the hundreds of lives that were lost in the seven train bombings in Mumbai.

I was well aware of the importance of teaching from the spirit world. The constant climbs in our learning curve are a part of the lifelong apprenticeship with spirit. There's no formal accreditation after the years of dedication to the spirit world. The trust and surrender of our lives that give credit to spirit and the healing provided to humanity is the ultimate outcome of all our hard work as mediums.

Luke, my housemate at the time, picked me up from the airport. I was pretty excited to see him as we always shared my spiritual experiences. Even though Luke is a police officer and considered to be quite rational, he has a very caring and open-minded nature with a left and right-brain balance similar to mine. He was raised in a small country town in New South Wales and he's still a country boy at heart, despite living in Sydney for almost 10 years now. I do not believe it was a coincidence that we moved to Sydney at almost exactly the same time and later met and became best friends. Our birthdays are days apart, too.

Luke is a very good-looking young man – being tall with blond hair and blue eyes. At times he gets away with a little more than usual by using his charm and charisma. We have a soul connection with one another that goes far deeper than most. We discuss everything and anything. Luke has a natural willingness to want to look at all players involved in any situation with an attempt to try and see the greater learning in it all. Not many people will admit it but it's much easier to blame an outer person before looking within. Like most people, Luke does indeed struggle with the learning of everyday life, however he constantly self-reflects in an attempt to become a better person each and every day. It is this power, the power of knowing the importance of ownership and responsibility, that I admire in him the most.

Arriving home from the airport late at night, Luke and I spoke at length about my trip in India. As we were drinking a cup of tea, I noticed that the bottom of my cup had a perfectly shaped elephant made from small tea-leaves. Lakshmi, a goddess from India, was associated with elephants, so we had a great laugh about the timing of it all.

The next day when I got to work, Vicki, my work colleague and friend, examined the photo I had captured in India. Vicki is an excellent photographer who has taken thousands of photos across the world and she takes her photography quite seriously. I needed a rational opinion and not long after that she confirmed that the photo was indeed real. Not only did she confirm this, she handed me a book on goddesses in India she'd been holding onto for a while.

I was pretty excited about this and knew that my tea incident the night before was just another confirmation. I do not share this photo with anyone now as I believe it was a special gift from the spirit world to me. The photo is just a reminder of the energetic bond that's created between the two worlds and the knowingness that anything is possible beyond the veil of spirit.

As I'm typing these words, I can't help but laugh at the possibilities of where those early days of the apprenticeship could have ended up. Those people who were part of this earlier journey later became great supporters in my work for spirit and I believe it was the evidence I provided to them that gave the spirits credibility and their proof of existence. This credibility was no longer to be shared just among family, friends and work colleagues but now to the public at large for mass healing purposes.

Over the next few weeks, I clearly heard the same radio station message over and over again in the mornings as I was waking up. Now this didn't come from a physical radio, given that I never had one switched on anyway. It was the same message most mornings and at different times and always when I was waking, so I knew it was the spirit world. My hearing senses with spirit are always very strong. I could hear the following message: *"Georgina connects with spirits from the other side, so call if you wish to communicate with your loved ones."*

I had no idea who Georgina was and to my own surprise I didn't feel compelled to investigate immediately. Like most things with spirit, timing is everything. One morning, I arrived in the office after a typical repeat radio message. It was a bit like the movie *Groundhog Day*, where the guy wakes up to the same scenario every morning. When I arrived at my desk there was a magazine article sitting there about a lady called Georgina. Vicki, my work colleague, had no idea about my repeating message but she thought I might be interested in the article since she knew about my experiences with the spirit world.

I realised then that if I didn't action this message sent from spirit, it would just continue. I decided to send Georgina an email to see if she could meet me as she was also a medium. Her website indicated that she was booked out, however she sent a reply message almost immediately asking for me to come. I was now intrigued and shared with Vicki that I was off to meet Georgina in a few days.

Georgina indicated that my gift of connecting with the spirit world would be shared with many people. It was time to take this communication forward and execute the work of spirit. As she was tuning into my energy, I felt I'd known Georgina before. There was a knowingness that we'd met one another, however, not in this lifetime. I began to tune into our connection and I could see us building up a friendship over a period of time.

I didn't share that information with Georgina at the time and after finishing the reading, she encouraged me to maintain contact with her via email. We regularly sent emails to one another, shared lunches and now she has become a great friend and supporter of my public mediumship work. It's good to have someone else to talk to who sees and hears spirit and still today we laugh about it all over our enjoyable lunches and dinners.

It was a June winter's morning and the anniversary of my grandmother's funeral. I was heading off to a centre in Western Sydney to share my mediumship with others. Luke was excited, too, and said I should definitely enjoy the day at "Hogwarts". As I drove for two hours to my destination, I reflected again on the meaning of life, or even death, like I always do when travelling long distances on my own. As I arrived at the centre, I was introduced to two mediums, Kerrie and Dianne.

Kerrie was a shorter lady with blonde hair and blue eyes, while Dianne was a little taller with brown hair and green eyes. Their energies were quite different, however, their own grief in life had brought them together as mediums. They always extended themselves out to people who were hurting from grief. They had some similarities in their backgrounds and I strongly believe their souls were brought together for significant reasons in this life. For me, their significance in my life was to help ignite the torch to assist me in sharing my gift of mediumship more with the public.

Kerrie asked me to sit with Dianne and conduct a reading for her. Now, this was the first time I had ever done such a thing. Could I just call upon the spirit world and ask them to speak to me? What an exciting challenge! Spirit always just seemed to start the conversation with me and most of the time finished it, too. I trusted that I was sent there for a reason, so I just surrendered myself and handed it over to the spirit world.

Immediately I was well aware of a gentleman in spirit with dark hair and he told me his name was "John Edward". Now, I didn't know whether this was a joke at first. John Edward is the name of an internationally renowned platform medium and here in my first reading was a spirit sharing the same name. He further confirmed this by showing me a gravestone and indicated he was Dianne's father. I started to relay this information and she nodded her head with confirmation of the evidence. Now I was excited – I had a name, description and passing of this man and proceeded to ask him more questions. The reading went very well and my confidence in the spirit world grew much further from that first official reading.

Dianne received lots of healing that day and we bonded together on a very deep level. Kerrie decided I would go under Dianne's wing as she could see we were similar in personality and energy. Dianne is a very easygoing person who sees the humour in most things in life, just like me. We would often laugh about the craziest things and always trusted that the spirit world would guide us in many ways. Dianne had a tragic upbringing with the suicide of her own father and the death of a brother and mother. Growing up in poverty and abuse, she managed to successfully raise a very functional family. I'm proud of her today for what she has achieved personally in life and I'm glad to still call her a dear friend.

Dianne will always be one of those close friends I call once in a blue moon and we just pick up where we left off. We have a mutual understanding that our lives are busy and we don't need to constantly be in contact with one another in the physical sense. I do often think of her and I know she's connecting with and supporting me on a spiritual level. I also often think of all the people who were there in the early days, when we called ourselves the "Wacky Wolves". I was always excited to drive the long distance to obtain greater learning from the spirit world and glad to provide healing to others. Even though we have now taken different paths, that chapter of my life was very special to me. The support and friendship from like-minded people – with a bit of fun as well – was a true gift from spirit that I will always be grateful for.

Throughout those exciting days of mediumship, I was introduced to a lovely lady by the name of Margareta. Her presence was unique. She had an aura filled with so much love for humanity it was evident in her energy. We were immediately drawn to one another. She was a natural-born healer, too. Soon, I allowed Margareta to conduct regular healing sessions on my body as my work intensity with the spirit world increased greatly. Every week we would spend time together, conducting healing and dreaming of opening our work up to the public on a greater level.

One evening, we decided to open her house up to the public for mediumship demonstrations. Margareta and I were very excited and we spent hours setting up our special little room. The residence was a house in Five Dock, Sydney (NSW) and we only had old chairs for the audience. Margareta decided to cover the chairs with white sheets to hide their age, as well as provide those sitting in the chairs with the pureness of white for healing energy. We also placed a little angel card on each of the seats so everyone got a message in some way. This system of covering chairs with white and having angel cards on every seat would become a trademark for all my future platform events.

I had never performed a public demonstration before, I had only ever worked one-on-one tuning into the spirits around an individual. A public demonstration would involve me tuning into the spirits in the room first and then, through the evidence provided by the spirits, a link would be made to their loved ones in the audience. Margareta had decided to tell a few of her close friends to come along for the first evening as part of the little experiment. I had no knowledge about these people at all – I had never met any of Margareta's friends or family. The only person I had met connected to Margareta was her husband, Ray. He was a complete sceptic and had no intention of getting involved in spirit stuff, so he was perfect to keep the experiment above board.

The first platform mediumship evening started with a few lovely songs to blend with the energy of the spirit world and I was immediately well aware of the spirits in the room. I could feel my spirit guides drawing close and I began my work. I had no time to even think or start to get nervous about it all and I just worked through the messages one by one. Supposedly the two things human beings fear most are public speaking and death. That evening I was combining the two for the first time, which was a great achievement in itself.

Looking back on my first platform evening, the spirits were definitely the ones doing all the talking and I just seemed to be going along with the healing. Over the years as a medium, you gain much stronger control over the energy of the room and learn to focus on one spirit at a time. You manage to tune out the hundreds or even thousands of other spirits while demonstrating.

But on that first evening, that was far from my worries. The spirit world was talking to me and I could make sense of the messages and relay the evidence to loved ones in the audience. The evening gave me a hunger for platform mediumship and ignited a flame inside of me. I knew in the moment I stood up, I had found my soul's purpose in life. I was here to teach humanity that there's more to life beyond physical death. I was excited and so was the spirit world and together we made a great team.

My spirit guides and I named our team between the two worlds "Team Spirit". This name would encapsulate all the helping souls involved in my work, including my guides in the spirit world. Once we had a name for our team, the work from the spirit world flowed very naturally, since our purpose was formally acknowledged. Humanity would be shown the evidence of life after death and no soul should ever leave the earth plane fearful of such a transition. No soul should ever worry where their loved ones were, regardless of whether they have a physical body. No soul should ever feel alone, for we are not alone but part of a connected universe that has no limits of time or space.

The day after our first platform evening, Margareta was bombarded with phone calls and soon our second evening was fully booked. Ray, Margareta's husband, was not impressed at all. Not only were there spooks in the back room of his house but living strangers as well, interfering with his quiet Friday evenings. On the second platform evening, Ray's father dropped in from the spirit world with a clear and precise message. He provided great evidence and with this I knew in my heart that Ray was a believer on some level. Ray is rational in thinking but also a kind-hearted soul. How he put up with Margareta, me and the public in those initial stages, I really don't know. He even made cups of tea for everyone at the end of the sessions – except for the spirits, of course!

It was only a short period of time before Margareta and Ray's house was overrun with people wanting to communicate with their loved ones on the other side. Maria, a gifted healer, was soon sent from the spirit world to assist Margareta with the rising public demands. I clearly recall the turning point when Ray had enough and decided we needed a larger premises to accommodate the public. There wasn't even enough room for him to sit in his own chair. Ray and Margareta booked the Community Centre down the road. That was the beginning of my regular large mediumship events and peace again for Ray on Friday nights, too.

The Community Centre was booked in advance for spirit communication evenings. Ray would help set up all the chairs and then take off for fish and chips and some peace and quiet back at home on those Friday nights. He would magically arrive back like a little angel at the end of the evening and help pack everything up. Today, the three of us have a good old laugh about those wonderful early days. When I told him I was writing this book, he hoped for a personal signed copy – and for me to never forget where it all started. That I won't forget and I'm sure he'll never forget either.

Chapter 5

Mechanics of Mediumship

Standing still can also be done sitting down.
Team Spirit

I'm a strong believer that it's healthy to be sceptical but not cynical – there's a big difference. Someone who's sceptical of anything in life has the ability to assess information placed in front of them and make a decision as to whether they wish to reassess previous thought processes. This is normal for any human being. I know that when I was three years of age, I truly believed I could jump off the back verandah and fly. It wasn't until some time later that I began to have an understanding that perhaps it wasn't physically possible. I began to reassess my thoughts. It was only through the explanation of the laws of physics that I could fully understand why it wasn't possible.

The same also applies to mediumship. If someone can physically stand up in a roomful of hundreds of people and give names, addresses, events and specific details of people's deceased loved ones, along with very personal details of their lives without having met them, I would definitely think twice as a sceptic or non-believer. Now, if I was less sceptical and more cynical, then very little further thought would be given to reassess current belief systems. My spirit guides on the other side have clearly explained the difference between a sceptic and a cynic.

A cynical person is someone who has no core belief systems. They do not have any level of understanding of where they have come from or who they are. They would not even be able to grasp the concept of connectivity in the universe as a cynical person is negative about everything in life. Not only are cynical people always negative, they lack enormous self-love and cannot see the beauty in most things in life. A cynical person will typically take the side of a debate that they see as winning. Most of the time, they're not even interested in the topic of discussion. This inability to process thought and reassess life in general prevents them from growing further in wisdom and knowledge. In terms of mediumship, how can a cynical person grasp the afterlife if they can't even be positive about their current life?

My guides often refer to the universe as a higher intelligence and they point out the amazement of life during my walks on the beach. So much universal energy is required to keep our planet warm and well-lit through the use of the sun. A massive amount of energy is required to move the tides through the influences of the moon cycles. Each and every cell in our body serves a purpose and the organs within every living thing have been built for a specific function. It's this purpose, the purpose of everything in the universe, that simply extends to our own lives.

If everything within you and around you serves a purpose, wouldn't it make sense that your life does, too? What would be the purpose of life, if life itself had no purpose? To believe that there's no higher level of intelligence than man would indicate some level of arrogance and ignorance. If man were the creator and the highest source of intelligence in the universe then why today can't we, with all the current technology, recreate bodies and organs when needed? It's this arrogance and ignorance that my guides believe fuels the cynical. These blocks in their minds prevent them from seeing the beauty within their own lives as well as the environment and inhabitants around them.

Scientific evidence today has proven that there is a higher level of consciousness and everything in the universe is connected through energy. If you research, you'll find thousands of articles on this topic. Studies on the subject of water have found that intense negative thoughts projected towards a glass of water, or a negative message written on the glass, over a couple of days will change its molecular structure. This structure will change dramatically again when classical music is played, or beautiful messages of love are written on the glass. If thoughts can change the structure of water molecules, then why wouldn't thoughts affect the health of our physical bodies, since they are mostly comprised of water?

If cynical souls cannot see the beauty of what's right in front of them each and every day, it would be very difficult for them to see the beauty and reality of the realms beyond. This is why it's so important that world leaders are not cynical, for they would have no concept of the consequences of their actions on humanity or the planet earth. If life serves no purpose at all, then the taking of lives and destruction through war could be done with ease. You can now see why it's healthy to be sceptical and not cynical – the difference is immense.

Throughout my years in mediumship, I've never really come across many hardcore cynical people. I've met many sceptics but I don't mind interacting with them. I've had some visitors at my mediumship events from sceptic organisations wishing to study or investigate my mediumship while I'm demonstrating. They look for sure signs, such as body language reading, but how far could that take the medium? A medium can't tell the names, description and personal events of their deceased loved ones in the spirit world just by looking at someone. I will always first describe the spirit with me on the platform with very specific details, including names and events, before even opening the reading up to the audience. However on many occasions, even the sceptics have no words for the work of the spirit world.

On at least five occasions, I've had a spirit with me on platform where the person I connected to in the audience had no idea the person had passed over. On such occasions, it's been a bit of a surprise for me as well since I always assume the audience will know who's on what side of life. Under these circumstances, generally the spirit person comes from overseas and news hasn't reached here yet, or they passed over after the commencement of the platform event. Either way, I personally believe it would be the best way to receive the news. I would know then for certain that my loved ones had arrived safely on the other side. I remember that on one such occasion, a sceptic from an association was in the audience and I'm sure this provided him with some significant teaching from the spirit world as well.

There have been other readings where it would be physically impossible for me as the medium to know the information coming through from the spirit world. I try not to give out warning messages to people in the audience. Why would the spirit world leave information with someone if they couldn't prevent or change the event? It would cause nothing but trauma for the sitter and would certainly not align with the healing purpose of mediumship. The spirit world will only provide a warning if the message serves a great healing or teaching purpose. On those few occasions, I see a large news flash from my spirit guides with a broadcast message coming through.

One evening, a broadcast warning message came through from my guides that practically stopped the platform. I was in the middle of a reading when they warned that the sister of the person I was reading would encounter danger in the next 15 minutes. My guides had indicated that a man would approach the front door of her sister's home. Her sister would open the door and the man would smash through the glass and harm himself. Her sister and the baby would be protected and no harm would come to them. Within 30 minutes of the reading all the information was confirmed – it happened exactly how my spirit guides had explained as well as the timing.

On another occasion, the spirit world provided a warning message to a lady in a very gentle and caring way. She was in the audience and her father came through from the spirit world. He indicated that there was a large amount of money stored in a location only known to her mother. Her mother hadn't shared this information with her. I had to be very careful giving the specific details publicly, so I provided everything except the address of her home.

Her father continued on in the reading, providing a specific date when he said there would be a large gathering of sad people. He said that personally, he couldn't wait for the big celebration! The lady in the audience said she'd be leaving for holidays on that day so there must have been an error in the date provided by her father. As usual, I explained to her that I could not edit or filter the information. That was what I was being told.

Around two weeks later, the same lady arrived at my platform and came to speak to me afterwards. She said her mother had passed away unexpectedly and the day indicated at the previous platform reading was the day of the funeral. Everyone else may have been sad that day, but her father was celebrating as he was together again with his soul mate. The details about the money being held behind the staircase were accurate, too. The contract date of her mother's life could not be changed. The spirit world attempted to prepare the daughter in a subtle way for her mother's transition.

One day I received a phone call to attend a television studio to meet some producers who were interested in making a psychic program. My guides encouraged me to go along as it would provide me with greater learning. When I arrived at the studio, the meeting room contained five men and two women, most of them television producers. I hadn't met these people before. All they knew was that I was recommended to demonstrate to them the mechanics of mediumship.

Immediately as I entered the room, I was well aware of an older gentleman in the spirit world standing next to me. Without hesitation, I started to relay the usual information such as names, descriptions, passing and so on. Once the spirit was clearly identified, he then asked me to connect to the guy in the group whose mother was changing her hairstyle and colour that morning. A young gentleman in the room raised his hand and confirmed the spirit as his grandfather. Apart from all the evidence, he had called his mother that morning and she mentioned she was having her hair done that day, so he knew I was definitely with him.

The grandfather in spirit had clearly identified himself to his grandson and provided proof that his consciousness had survived physical death. He had given an observation of an event on that day, as well as many other events and details. The normal structure of my readings is to provide identification of the spirit, proof of consciousness and a healing message. The young man was attentive as his grandfather gave him a warning message. He told him that upon his return to Los Angeles, there would be a serious incident involving his vehicle. He provided very specific details of the crime. He told his grandson that he would be protected and not to worry when the situation arose.

I left the studio that day knowing that the spirit world had deliberately planted a seed of some sort for the producers. I rarely give out predictions on platform unless it serves a higher purpose of either teaching or healing. Within a couple of weeks, I received a phone call from another producer from the studio saying that the young gentleman I had read was subjected to the exact crime that was described in detail in his reading that day and he was protected. Even though *they* were shocked and surprised, *I* certainly wasn't stunned. The spirits are always correct. If his grandfather could provide so many details with accuracy and they were validated immediately on the day, why wouldn't the last part of the reading come to fruition as well? The spirit world is not limited by time, so they are able to bring through events into this world that have not yet happened.

So in all these circumstances, how does the medium obtain information not only about the recipient's loved ones in the spirit world but also their current lives and future events in their lives here on earth? If the recipient doesn't know the information yet, how can they give these details off in body language? The answer is simple – it's impossible. My spirit guides have said that if such body language information could be read, the divorce rates in the world would be extremely low. People could just go to parties and immediately find the love of their lives and view their future happiness by simply looking at how these people sit in their chairs or stand in a certain way.

If it were at all possible to obtain current and future events through reading body language, I'm sure a billion-dollar business would have been created by now. On the opposite side of love, if this were at all possible, psychologists could determine details of a murder, such as where the body was hidden and names and details, just by observing the perpetrator sitting in a chair. The theory of obtaining all this information through body language seems quite ridiculous. So how do mediums get their information?

The easiest way to explain mediumship is through vibrational frequencies. Think of a radio receiver tuning into various radio stations. Most people here on earth are focused on the earth radio station, since their purpose in life is to obtain an experience here on earth and then move over into the spirit world when their physical life has been completed. However, if the vibrational frequency of the soul is much higher, it will have the ability to tune into other stations and bring forward information from other realms of existence.

The earth plane has one of the lowest vibrational frequencies in the universe. When energy vibrates at a very slow rate it bonds together to form physical matter. This is why the earth plane is a physical world. The physical bodies we reside in also vibrate at this lower frequency so we can manage to have an experience in this world. Outside the physical body is another energy field known as the aura. Your aura contains a unique fingerprint of your energy and your own consciousness.

When your physical body no longer functions through death, you will simply move into your aura or spirit body energy field and reside on another plane of existence. These other planes of existence vibrate at much higher frequencies and there's a faster vibration in your spirit body to match this new living environment. Your spirit body can survive in the spirit world since you no longer require your surroundings to be vibrating much more slowly in order to produce physical matter.

This is why your loved ones in the spirit world will never starve, be cold or feel physical pain. These are physical characteristics of the physical body on a physical earth plane. Whether your body is physical or etheric (spirit), it will live in the plane of existence according to its vibrational frequency. If the soul is full of love, light and wisdom through connectivity, it will reside at higher levels of existence in the spirit world.

When a medium walks into a room, they have the ability to adjust their energy when focusing on multiple planes of existence. They can turn the knob a little higher or lower and the adjustment of the vibrational frequency of their senses can be attuned. Someone who is not attuned would simply walk into a room and not see or feel anyone else around them from other planes of existence. Adjustments of this frequency by the medium allows them to connect to different energies at different frequencies. So in a room full of many living people, they may be the only living person attuning to loved ones in the spirit world. It's like the medium has the ability to adjust a dimmer light in the room and they can see and feel spirit while most people in the room have the light switched off.

When loved ones in spirit make a connection with me, my vibrational frequency is connecting higher into the spirit world and your loved ones in spirit will lower their frequency. There will be a process of blending our energies together until the tuning of the transmitter has been achieved. Once we have blended our energies, we will then use my senses to bring forward information through the mechanics of mediumship.

The five main physical senses are seeing, hearing, feeling, touch and taste. Once the spirit begins to send information through, I receive it through my five main spiritual senses. The first sense is clairvoyance, meaning clear seeing. I see a vision or a flash of pictures like a movie in front of me, in my third eye. Together with clairvoyance, I normally hear words or sounds through clairaudience. Hearing is one of my strongest senses as well as vision. This information is further enhanced through clairsentience, where I personally feel the emotions of the spirit in the situation I'm experiencing at the time.

The fourth sense that I find fascinating is claircognisance. This is where I unexpectedly receive a very quick download of an event and all its details in a split second. I didn't see anything, hear or even feel it but just know it to be important information and truth. It feels like a microchip of information has been placed in my head with an instant download. On rare occasions, I can taste and smell through the senses of spirit.

After the medium has blended with the spirit, information is then received at the same or different times through various senses. The interpretation of the information now begins. I believe this is the greatest skill of the medium. It would be like buying a television set that's been tuned to the western world and then attempting to use it in a developing country. Not all the sounds and pictures come through clearly without the correct blending of energy and interpretation of the spirit.

To allow those in the developing countries to understand what a western world movie on the television set is all about, a good interpreter is required to put the words and pictures together and provide the feeling and emotion of the movie. The same also applies to mediumship. The medium is the television set transmitting information between two worlds. Different spirits use different senses, so the messages will vary from spirit to spirit just like the television set will vary when plugged in from country to country here on earth. Over time, the medium obtains a greater level of understanding of the mechanics of mediumship and can adjust their energy according to the vibrational frequency of the spirit energy.

When I'm demonstrating in front of a large audience, I can immediately feel the overall vibrational frequency of the room when entering. I have a level of knowingness of how much additional energy may be required for the evening for sufficient blending with the spirit world. If the audience feels flat or depressed, the medium may need to work harder to obtain a clearer connection with the spirit world. Either way, I am never too hard on myself as I can only give as much energy as physically possible. I remember one evening my guides saying to me: *"Man has only physically travelled as far as the moon and he did not receive clear pictures and sounds with all that technology. You receive clear pictures and sounds on your own with one physical body across two worlds of existence. This in itself is a true gift for all involved."*

Chapter 6

Bridging Two Worlds as One

Why are areas of the world that are physically starved more spiritually nourished?
Team Spirit

After hundreds of audience demonstrations and thousands of readings, I'm still amazed at how mediums communicate with another world. In the previous chapter, I attempted to explain my understanding of the mechanics of mediumship. However, in addition to that, perhaps the most important anchor in this is the dedicated team of spirit helpers and guides on the other side, in the spirit world. I openly refer to this team as "Team Spirit", for they are a very important part of, not only *my* life, but *your* life, too, when you obtain healing through any of the work that I present to you, including this book.

For me, Team Spirit is very sacred and it has taken years to build and trust in our relationships with one another. These beings of light are responsible for all the tests I've been through, the guidance in my work and bringing forward your loved ones and wisdom into this world. I believe that true mediumship is impossible without this help. Not only would the medium be bombarded with thousands of spirits, there would be less wisdom to share since a lot of inspiration and knowledge is given from the higher realms.

Over the years, I have worked with many guides serving different purposes. The main energies I have worked with are known as Avalon, Sabash and Punyu. Avalon is of Native American descent and has a great deal of wisdom and knowledge to share with humanity. He is a very loving and caring soul and also a strong believer in sharing life experiences with one another. The first time he presented himself to me, he gave me a lovely gift of beads in a wonderful spiritual vision. My living healing team have got to know him from this side of the veil as well through me.

Sabash is also very strong in his healing abilities and quite different to Avalon. He's a small, ancient Chinese man with grey hair and a beard. He loves me dearly and tends not to talk too much. He just arrives and does the work that needs to be done. The first evening I met him I was very upset about something and to my surprise he appeared very solid in my room, offering a possible solution. We are so different in looks and personality, however we always work very well together. He has taught me the art of discipline and focus of the mind. He reminds me a lot of the older man in *The Karate Kid* – that's the best way for me to describe him.

My Aboriginal healing guide is nicknamed "Punyu" and she has been with me for some years now. She is a very loving soul and we have a deep understanding for one another on many levels.

There are three other main guides who I work with on a regular basis, however Avalon, Sabash and Punyu have been the main ones. I try not to talk too much about my guides' personalities, as guides over the years do change and they too have a life of their own in the spirit world. I respect this greatly. I know that some people in the spiritual community talk about having guides of different origins and descents. We need to remain grounded when it comes to discussing spirit guides from the spirit world.

My belief is that the more advanced souls would only draw close to the earth plane for teaching or healing purposes. You won't find them hanging out all day with people here on earth for fun or pleasure; they have moved beyond the interests of earth life and serve a greater teaching purpose for humanity. If the person on this side is not healing or teaching through the work of the spirit world, then there would be no purpose or desire for the more advanced souls to be around. This brings up the topic of intention that I strongly believe is an important part of the spirit world relationship.

When a group of spirit guides decides to work with a medium, there needs to be a likeness in energy for the blending to occur. The intention of the medium needs to be aligned with the guides' intentions. It is the blending of the medium with their guides that forms the initial bridging together of the two worlds. The higher the vibrational frequency of the medium through love and light, the greater the variance of spirit energies they can blend with on the other side. Apart from connecting you to your loved ones in the spirit world, massive amounts of wisdom and knowledge from entities of higher realms can be brought through the medium to people on this side of life. Humanity can then obtain not only healing through readings, they can also raise their own soul consciousness through universal love and knowledge.

In the early stages of my public audience demonstrations, there was an increase in the recruitment of living helpers by Team Spirit on this side of the bridge. On one such occasion, I was demonstrating at Margareta's for the last time and the room was so full we had to move the additional furniture outside so I could demonstrate in the corner of the room. I remember one reading very clearly. I've never felt so odd, stuck as I was in the corner of the room with three young male spirits.

The first spirit to come through identified himself clearly as Bill. The young man was wearing a nice suit and showed me how he had passed through heart failure after battling lung cancer for a short period of time. He was very charismatic and good-looking and soon his charm had the interest of not only his sister Kat, who was in the audience, but me as well. She couldn't believe he was coming through as he had only passed 17 days earlier. Being a natural giver, Kat had brought someone else along that night for healing and didn't expect a reading for herself. I hadn't met Kat before, so the first time we spoke was through Bill's reading.

Bill not only gave excellent evidence of his survival, he then brought forward two other men who were his friends on this side of life who passed tragically within weeks of his own transition. One young gentleman who stepped forward had passed as a result of a boating accident. The vision I could see on platform was identical to a clear vision I had seen many months before, however this man had only just passed over. Another young man then stepped forward. He had been shot and killed in Greece. These two other men were Bill's mates on the earth plane and together the three of them boasted about standing near each other's coffins at their own funerals.

Bill really had the audience laughing with his larrikin behaviour when he wrote up his age in front of me. It didn't seem right at all as he wrote up 53 and was laughing his head off. I told his sister what I was seeing – it seemed to be unbelievable to me – and she said that he was dyslexic and his age was actually 53 backwards. Bill passed over into the spirit world at 35 years of age.

At the end of the reading, Kat asked Bill why he had not shown himself to her before. Unexpectedly, Bill responded by asking Kat why she had made no effort in showing herself to him in his world. I was surprised at his response and thought that he had raised a very valid point. I've been over to the spirit world many times (which I will discuss later on in the book). It's easy for people to place expectations on their loved ones to communicate with them once they've crossed over and mediumship in itself is a very difficult task for the spirits to achieve.

Spirit communication involves a large amount of energy. A great deal of effort is required by the spirits in an attempt to make a connection. Not only do they need to know how to communicate with the medium, they need to be able to recognise symbols, sounds and images that the medium can then interpret to obtain a full, clear message. On top of all this, much guidance needs to be given by them to place you in front of me in the first place. That's a lot of effort for someone who no longer lives in the same world as you.

Through Bill's reading, Kat became one of my dear helpers at platform and we have formed a close friendship over the years. She's a natural-born healer, as noted by my guides that evening and if it were not for Bill's passing into spirit, her path may have been quite different in life. She nursed and provided healing to her brother Bill right up until the end, which no doubt opened her heart to new levels of compassion. This, in time, would be of assistance to many other people experiencing grief.

One evening, an audience member gave me an angel statue as a gift of gratitude. I also received a bunch of feathers from another person on a separate occasion. A few days later, Bill arrived in spirit to show me that the feathers needed to be placed on the angel statue's head and asked if the gift could be given to his father, Kon. I had no idea what it meant, so I just executed the message by giving the statue to Kat to give to Kon, from Bill. Kon was surprised as he'd had a spirit drawing done that week, of an angel who was a Native American. This no doubt confirmed to Kon that Bill was definitely around. Bill's Mum, Engela, has now also become a very dear friend, healer and helper to the spirit world.

I'm a strong believer in the greater plan of life. The vision of the man who passed in the boating accident occurred months before the accident actually happened and then Bill brought him through platform. Bill and the other men had not yet passed at the time of my vision those many months before. I believe that it was destined for these boys to pass at that time and why I was seeing the vision so far ahead was an indication of the assistance that was to come from the spirit world in the form of Kat and Engela.

It was part of Kat and Engela's life path to work as helpers and healers for the spirit world. Bill was important in opening up that path, just like my brother was when I was little. This was further confirmed to me when I met another special friend and healer, Elke, who had also lost her brothers and father. I met Elke within weeks of meeting Kat and the two of them have become important pillars on this side of the bridge in assisting with the work of the spirit world. They tirelessly help me set up the events, as well as provide comfort and healing to those in need.

Shortly after meeting Margareta, Maria, Kat, Engela and Elke, spirit brought forward another important earthly helper. I was demonstrating to a group of people on a very hot evening and the session was almost over when a young boy who had passed in a car accident came through from the spirit world. The boy's mother didn't want to own up initially, however through persistence I encouraged her to work with me. She had been blaming herself for his death. The boy proceeded to provide great evidence from his world and made it known that he was fine and happy with his new life. He also shared an interesting experience he had the night before he passed. He had dreamt that he died and woke up wanting to tell the family. The boy went back to bed and of course the next day his dream had come true.

There was a middle-aged gentleman in the room that night who was intrigued by what was happening. He didn't say much and simply gave me a sandwich at the end of the evening and left. Some weeks later I saw him again when I was reading for a second mother who was full of grief and guilt. A small baby, who accidentally suffocated in her mother's arms, came through from the spirit world. The mother was very tired one morning, so the child's grandmother nursed the baby for a while. After a short time, the grandmother returned the baby to her mother's bed for a nap while she was sleeping. With no warning, the baby suffocated and passed into the spirit world. The message that evening was very healing – the mother became pregnant again not too long after the passing of the baby.

Looking back at the readings of those two separate grieving mothers, I can see the reason why the middle-aged man was sent to me. His name is Mayner and today he plays a very important part in the work of spirit. Shortly after these readings, he would just appear at the end of my audience demonstrations and pack up the chairs and leave. He didn't say much at all and just came and went like an angel. At first no-one really knew who he was and it took some time for him to start to open up more to the helpers. He even brought cake from his cafe that he runs seven days a week.

In a conversation with Mayner a few years later, I asked him why he had been so drawn to my work and to be of such great assistance to spirit. He mentioned three incidents that had occurred in his life that changed his outlook greatly. The first was that not long before I met him at the initial platform evening, he had suffered a serious heart attack that shook him up quite a bit. Not only did he have a heart attack, he also had pneumonia and almost certainly nearly lost his life. He had always been a spiritual man and now was more conscious of healing himself as well as others.

The second and third incidents were quite different. A lady used to come into Mayner's cafe every day asking if he would be open on Christmas Day. He had indicated to her on many occasions that he would not be opening and he started to get a little impatient with her. He thought he had made it clear that he was open most days but not that day. After he returned from his short Christmas break, he found out that the woman had jumped from the top of a building and taken her own life – on Christmas Day. This caused him a great deal of pain.

The third incident occurred when Mayner decided to invite a young man, a friend of a friend, to a football game. He spent hours with the young man, bought him a bottle of water and chatted with him for a while. Not long after, Mayner found out that the young man had taken his own life – with no warning or signs at all. He felt like he had failed the young man – he wondered why he hadn't picked up on anything – and he carried guilt from that incident as well. Two people had taken their lives and this kind man felt a level of guilt like they were under his watch.

It's only now, while I'm writing this book, that spirit has informed me of the link with Mayner from the beginning. He was present when two women felt the guilt of the loss of their children, with the belief that their actions could have changed the paths of them crossing over. This was no different to how Mayner felt about the loss of the lady and the young man through suicide. He was placed in front of the two mothers to witness the guilt-driven pain other people feel and to bring forward his own self healing. The solution for Mayner was then to assist others with grief. He would show that we can take something that most would consider to be a negative experience and see it as a positive learning one. Mayner had taken on board the learning that was given to him and thus decided to dedicate a part of his life to helping others heal through the work of the spirit world.

I have never felt as though this work was given to me to execute on my own. In the beginning, most of the time I was simply building a bridge to the other side with the assistance of Team Spirit. Once the pillars were built on both ends, the spirits began their journey back and forth in some sort of pre-ordained order. I imagine this bridge to be like a wooden swing bridge that has rope handles on the sides. Sometimes the spirits would find it hard to connect. Once their vibrations were attuned enough to meet mine, I could take their hand and bring them forward. There would be times when I felt perhaps a little wobbly for the two of us but we always managed to hang on together and get the message through to their loved ones.

Looking back at the early days of platform, I now know there were a few more spirits hanging onto the bridge and rope than perhaps there should have been. One spirit attempting to make a connection will use the energy of others to adjust their vibration. They would start to connect and then other relatives on the other side would group their energy together and the bridge would perhaps sway a little. Once they knew I had hold of a few hands, they all were confident enough to bring forward their messages.

The problem with working with multiple spirits like this is that a few would want to talk at the same time and that can be confusing for the medium. It took some discipline from me and my spirit guides to get some level of order on the bridge. Now when a couple of people walk over, I balance the energy and try to take over only one person at a time. If I'm aware of a group of people, I ask my guides to assist in choosing the best spokesperson for the group.

Normally, it's the person who can blend the easiest with the medium. This doesn't mean the other relatives and friends on the other side are not involved. They're helping by giving encouragement, energy and bits of other evidence for the reading. On occasion, they may call out their names and I'll repeat them to the person who's being read. Some of the time, I'll describe who the other spirits are as well.

I do love working with spirits who make their way over the bridge. I really do and it gives me a great level of excitement and gratitude even now as I'm sharing this with you. I always feel it a privilege that they've chosen me to be their spokesperson, their voice. It carries with it a great level of responsibility and I always do my best to represent who they are and bring forward evidence and healing to their loved ones on this side of life.

I never give up on the spirit people; I'm known publicly to be very persistent on platform. These people are making a lot of effort to get a message through to someone and there's no way I will hang up the phone line on them that easily. It's not a joke, a game or entertainment. Mediumship is used for healing and so this is my primary intention when I'm executing a message to the sitters in the audience.

I've had many instances where someone is embarrassed by the spirit coming through or doesn't want to talk to them. No-one on this side of life determines who comes through – it's the spirit world's decision. If you attend a platform wishing to speak to someone in particular, there are no guarantees it will happen. There's a saying I always give at the start of any platform mediumship event: *"You will get what you need and not what you want."* If Team Spirit are aware of some unfinished business with someone, healing that's required for the spirit, or a greater level of teaching and healing for the audience, then this is what will be executed on platform.

The primary purpose of the spirit world is to remind each and every soul in front of them that life does goes on. There's no difference between the living spirits sitting in chairs in the audience and those behind me on platform. One spirit is incarnated into a physical body and the other is not. Energy can never be destroyed, only transformed. If you boil water it will evaporate into steam, or if you subject it to severe coldness it will freeze. The energy of the water can never be destroyed – it will always exist in some form or another. The same applies to all universal energy, including your loved ones. Energy is energy and spirit is spirit. So, all in all, there is no death but only transition into another world.

Chapter 7

There is No Death

A lighthouse remains a constant beacon of light for all seeking directional guidance by simply standing still and not judging those in need.
Team Spirit

When someone sheds their physical body here on earth, just like a snake sheds its skin, many people describe the process simply as someone has passed away. But where have they passed through? The word "passed" indicates moving beyond something to somewhere else. If the human race didn't believe in the afterlife on some deeper level, then why would such a transitory word be used so widely for this physical death process?

As a medium, it's not even questionable to me what happens when we die. The personality or the consciousness of the person who has passed over simply inhabits its energy into its spirit body, which vibrates at a higher frequency. This higher frequency resides in another world or dimension where life continues on just like it does here on earth. One of the most distinguished differences of these lives is truth. The personality of the person in spirit will now live in a world of truth. This is why I always trust what the spirit people tell me – I know they are speaking from truth. They have never tricked me or told me information that's untruthful or misleading.

There have been instances where people have been in the audience and not initially owned up to the spirit with me on the platform. I find this more common among males than females, as their sceptical, rational minds kick in, refusing to accept that there actually is someone here from the spirit world wishing to speak to them. I find that the spirits themselves can feel rejected and lose confidence and only through encouragement from me will they continue to stay connected. These spirits are people as well, with feelings and emotions just like they had here on earth and sometimes it's easy for people to forget this.

One evening I had a male spirit with me who provided what I thought was excellent evidence. He gave his name, location and exact description of death. He even called out the last few words he said before he died so the man in the audience, who he had also named, would quickly identify him. The spirit was very persistent and I stayed with him for a good 10 minutes while there was silence in the audience. No-one owned up to him. It was only then, through desperation, that the spirit began to provide very personal information about the man in the audience and then he finally raised his hand.

The audience sighed with disbelief as the man validated all the information that had been given thus far. The male spirit became very excited and proceeded to provide further great evidence that he had continued living on the other side. The man he had wanted to speak to was involved in his death through an accident and felt an enormous amount of guilt through his passing. The man in spirit wanted to acknowledge the fact that his death could not have been prevented and it wasn't the living man's fault. The man in the audience became very emotional as the healing between them continued throughout the reading. It moved the audience immensely as well.

There was another instance where I saw a male spirit desperate to communicate with his mate in the audience. I remember the reading very clearly as I could feel the determination of the spirit wanting to communicate a message to his wife. His wife wasn't in the audience but there was a male work colleague who had the potential to pass the message on. The male spirit had been involved in a work accident where a concrete construction had collapsed and killed him instantly. His family had witnessed the accident, causing a great level of stress and trauma to everyone involved.

He provided great evidence of his identification and passing and then proceeded to provide specific details of an incident that had occurred to his work colleague the week before platform. He named the exact location where one of the work trucks had a tyre blowout, including the date and time. This was surely enough evidence to the man in the audience that this was his work mate and that he had indeed survived physical death and was continuing to observe his work colleagues from another world. He also asked the man to visit his wife and children and give them a bunch of flowers on his behalf. I have no doubt that the reading was very healing for both men involved, as well as their families.

As I'm writing this chapter, my thoughts are taken immediately to a man in the spirit world who wanted to communicate with his grandson in the audience. This spirit man loved his grandson dearly and was determined to get a message to him, no matter what. As I proceeded to provide evidence to the audience, I was aware of a group of teenagers in the crowd who were laughing out loud. I have no doubt they had come along intrigued about what went on at a spirit communication evening. Somehow it was no longer a laughing matter when the spirit of the grandfather gave direct evidence to whom he wanted to speak.

Reluctantly, a young man raised his hand, acknowledging that the man in spirit was indeed his grandfather. As the teenagers were laughing, the grandfather began to speak to his grandson in a very direct, evidential manner. He stated the exact amount of money that had been lost by the teen through gambling and named the specific poker machine it had been lost on only hours before he attended the platform evening. The teenagers were stunned as this was immediately validated and they began to listen to the grandfather's words like it was their own grandad.

The young man was seen through the eyes of his grandfather as someone very special. He saw his grandson as someone who had great potential in life and also the potential to go off in the wrong direction without the correct guidance. He provided specific evidence of other silly things the boy was involved in and also the job opportunity phone message that had come to him that afternoon. He acknowledged the boat that was stolen just after he passed and the importance of this boat to his grandson as part of his inheritance.

This grandfather made a deal with his grandson just before he passed that he would show him a sign that he had arrived okay in the spirit world by knocking over a picture frame in the house. The problem was that he went one step further. He came through my platform wearing a picture frame around his head when he first introduced himself with specific names and details. I initially had no idea what the frame meant. Even though the young man's friends may have been laughing, it meant the world to the boy that his grandad had fulfilled his promise.

Not only did his grandfather frame his reading for him, a report was placed in the local newspaper that the boat was stolen and the young man was offered a new boat from the public. The love between these two males bridged the worlds together closely that evening and moved both me and the audience once again. I know that all the young people in the group that night had gained something great through the reading. It reminded them all that the elderly influential people in their lives may deteriorate in physical form but they will never leave them in thought. They will continue to guide them throughout their testing times and provide them with unconditional love and truth.

I always find a difference in communication between a male and female spirit on the platform. Of course, their personalities don't change when they move into the spirit world, so their attributes of how they communicate don't change either. On this side of life, a male spirit would generally identify himself clearly through facts, events and observations, perhaps on a more rational basis than a female. For this, they make greater evidential communicators, as I find that even though they may not have believed in the afterlife here on earth, they are excellent messengers when providing proof that there is an afterlife. Female spirits, on the other hand, sometimes need to be prompted by me to provide more concrete evidential facts instead of emotional details.

There was one instance of a spirit that I can clearly recall on platform. He was from overseas and his son was in my audience not knowing what to expect when the spirit world wanted to speak to him. His father not only identified himself clearly, he provided very specific evidence of a flight plan his son had booked on the computer days earlier. The son had also changed the flight plan and the spirit proceeded to relay the exact original and changed flight details, including the days and airport destinations. I was even surprised at his level of detail. The son wasn't, as he knew it was exactly how his father had operated in life here on earth.

As a female communicating information through for a male spirit, I find that I have many advantages of being born female and working in a more male-dominated line of work as a computer engineer. I am able to understand the emotions of a female spirit and also the more rational thinking side of a male spirit. I believe it's the balance of providing both evidence and a healing message of love that's of importance in any mediumship reading.

There are times when the spirits only provide excellent specific evidence of names, events and locations and I need to ask them to begin to provide a loving, healing message to balance out the reading. For some of the male spirits this can be difficult, especially if they did not communicate that well on this side of life. I know they wish to say something and they're not sure how to express it through words of love. In these instances, most of the time they will give an observation of something that perhaps they didn't pay much attention to in life. For instance, I remember a father giving an observation of a tool his son had picked up in his shed on a specific day that had meant a lot to him in life. His son was going through a tough time and this somehow bonded them together again on a much deeper level.

Females, on the other hand, mostly don't have problems in speaking to the medium. Sometimes they bring along other female spirits for support and this requires some discipline on my part. I find that here in life, females tend to talk about things in a more roundabout way in a group. In the spirit world, where there's no concept of time, intervention is sometimes called upon by the medium. I have had many instances where strong personalities of older women have come through the platform and they're determined to speak to their loved ones in the audience. There are times when two strong women come through and when I ask for one person at a time there's a pause while they squabble about who's going first!

I find that many women spirits in my mediumship provide some very personal observations of what's going on with people on this side of life. They tend not to exclude many people in their readings and they will call upon specific events with detail to prove they were there to observe them. I know that male spirits were at these events as well, that's not disputable, however females will want to talk about it more afterwards, just like they did here on earth. The specific details they provide to their friends, children, parents and grandchildren will always move their loved ones. It is this nurturing side of women that wishes for their loved ones to know they're providing support and comfort from the spirit world, without limitations.

I remember a reading one evening where the lady in spirit passed on the day of her daughter's wedding. The passing of a mother is a tragic event for any daughter to deal with but for it to happen on your wedding day the grief would be immense. The mother came through the platform, clearly identifying who she was and that she wished to communicate with her daughter. To her daughter's surprise, she described the rescheduled wedding event in detail and explained that she did everything from her side of life to make it a special day. Her daughter knew her mother had been with her in spirit on the new wedding day and had no idea how much input she had from the other side. Together they shared a special moment as her proud mother informed the audience of the power of the afterlife and how love can never separate us, no matter how tragic the circumstances may be. Her daughter's wedding day was important to her here on earth and continued to be so in the spirit world.

I believe that our loved ones protect and guide us in the spirit world far more than they could physically have done here on earth. They're no longer limited by time and space and when they hear you crying for help in your mind, they can immediately respond to your thoughts. One evening, a lady spirit came onto the platform wishing to communicate with her daughter and she had a sense of urgency. After the mother had clearly identified herself and made the connection, her daughter knew she had come with some strong healing advice. She had been living in a very abusive relationship and felt she had no way out of the physical threats and toxic environment. The spirit world is well aware that you are here of your own free will and they can't make decisions for you.

The mother recalled the terrible circumstances that she, too, had lived with for many years. She explained that only through the facing of her own death through illness did she come to terms with life choices. She gave her daughter encouragement that she would assist her from the other side if she made the choice to leave. She would guide her in a way that would provide peace to her daughter and grandchildren and they wouldn't need to face it all on their own again. She would continue to look over their shoulders no matter how harsh life might be and whatever decision her daughter did make she would never judge her. I have no doubt that the young woman in the audience made the right choice for both herself and her children with the continued guidance from her mother on the other side.

Not only did the reading provide healing for the daughter and her mother, it also provided healing to other women who came up to me afterwards in similar circumstances saying they felt as though they had regained their power. They had on some level also felt like they had physically died. But there is no death. We are all living spirits that have the free will to lead the lives we truly deserve. No matter how tough life may be, there is someone, somewhere in spirit form, either on this side of life or the other side, watching over your spirit.

Chapter 8

Healing Hands

Trust and truth all start with your true self.
Team Spirit

I often talk about the importance of healing in my work on all three levels: physical, mental and spiritual. This is the driving force behind all the work I do, as the intention of my mediumship is for healing purposes only. This is why I always say to people, *"You will get what you need and not what you want."* There's so much truth in this statement as true healing will be given to the soul at a much deeper level and will not necessarily satisfy the human ego wants of an individual.

One beautiful winter morning, I was walking with my sister Therese along a white sandy beach on the north coast of New South Wales. We were there over the weekend for a wedding, so we decided to enjoy the wonderful weather and scenic surroundings. As we walked, I received a clear message from the spirit world to collect some stones that had been washed to the shore for the next platform evening to be held in Sydney. I had no idea why and could see no reasoning for this but, as always, I trusted my spirit team. Therese and I collected lots of small stones along the beach and once we'd finished we looked at one another laughing! We wondered what it was all about as we struggled to carry the stones to the car.

After a wonderful weekend away, I returned to Sydney and prepared for my next audience demonstration. I had all the stones with me and I told Margareta and Maria we would be using them in meditation. Every person in the audience would be holding a stone in meditation. They trusted me and after a few hours of spirit communication with the audience, the evening was closed by a wonderful meditation guided by Margareta and Maria. I was sitting in a chair at the front of the room in an altered state of consciousness feeling as though I was about to go into a trance state.

Trance is an altered state of consciousness whereby the energy of my team in the spirit world can impress the medium to the extent where they have greater control over my mind and body. I'm a very experienced trance medium, so I know that the spirit world would only bring this type of mediumship forward to the public if it served a far greater purpose than the usual form of spirit communication. I have not undertaken a full trance state publicly since this incident which shows the importance of it that evening. At this stage, I could feel myself slipping under an anaesthetic type state and one of my spirit guides stepping forward to address the audience. Within seconds, my vocals projected to the audience with angelic sounds of healing and various tunes of frequency from my physical body.

By now, Margareta and Maria became very much aware of a young lady in the audience reacting to the sounds that were projecting. The young lady had breast cancer and she could feel healing energy penetrating her body and releasing the negative energy. The audience was surprised at the healing that was going on and could all feel the energy drawing through the stones while connecting one another in the audience. Trisha, the young lady receiving healing, remained very calm while this was occurring and within five minutes the healing meditation had come to a close.

Once I returned to my normal state of consciousness, I was surprised to hear so many people talking in the audience and attempting to convince me that something had just happened. I am the medium, the one always demonstrating to the audience and providing evidence of things far greater than the physical form. There was now a role reversal going on – the audience convincing the medium that something had occurred. Given I was in an altered state of consciousness and not aware of what had happened, I had to rely on the words of the hundred or so people in front of me.

I asked two of the men sitting near Trisha what had happened, as they seemed to be quite rational businessmen. They both said they felt an enormous pull across their body, towards Trisha, as if they were helping to provide energy for a healing of some sort. They said their stones had heated up and they felt they were connected to everyone in the audience. When I asked Trisha what had happened, she said she felt an enormous amount of energy coming from me towards her and entering her body and clearing negative energy. What surprised us all next was her story of an event that had occurred the previous week.

Even though Trisha and I had never met or crossed paths before, a week earlier we had both been standing on a beach, hundreds of kilometers away from one another, holding stones. While I was on the beach collecting the stones, Trisha had thrown a stone out to the ocean in Sydney and said to God: *"If you can hear me and I have the chance to survive all of this, the stone will come back to me."* The stone did come back to Trisha, and to all of us, in an amazing way that evening.

That evening, I made a decision to bring together a few of my helpers and Trisha to Margareta's house the following week to see if we could replicate the healing. It did indeed replicate and this was the formation of our healing group. We had no idea where it would lead but we were excited at the possibility of providing trance healing to those in need. I was willing to surrender myself to spirit for the new work and trusted that they would bring forward the people and premises to make it all possible.

The healing group soon expanded to include Margareta, Maria, Kat, Engela and Elke. It was no coincidence that spirit had brought them on board and of course Mayner was present at each of the sessions. The healing evenings began with a little meditation and then I would move into a trance state with spirit, and healing would be provided to those in need.

After a couple of weeks of the healing sessions, another lady who had cancer joined the group. Her name was Maddalena and she was brought to us by her sister, Roberta. Roberta was keen on helping the group and she became actively involved in assisting those in need. I remember one evening meeting a lady similar to Roberta by the name of Anastasia and her enthusiasm towards our work was immense. She was a natural-born giver with the art of hugging others she hadn't met before. She kindly offered her premises in the evenings for the work of spirit and so we found ourselves healing in a wonderful antique furniture store where the setting was just perfect.

Once a fortnight on a Wednesday, Anastasia would greet us with her dear friend Franca as we arrived for the healing evening. Franca is also a professional healer and together the two of them were a package in disguise. One would give all the hugs and kisses and the other would provide the reassurance to those in need that everything would be okay. The evening would conclude with wonderful Italian and Greek cakes. Those evenings are without doubt some of the fondest memories I have of working with spirit. We all trusted in my guides and we all took care of one another. And of course, I loved the cakes too.

Like any work for the spirit world, new learning involves new lessons and perhaps painful experiences in order to understand the workings of life in general. Both Trisha and Maddalena were doing well and their recoveries from cancer were under way. One evening at platform, after a spirit demonstration, a man by the name of Peter came up to me and asked if he could join the healing group. He was extremely unwell and I could see by the discolouration of his skin that he had advanced stages of liver cancer. He had barely any energy and even found it difficult to stand for a few minutes just to speak to me. The doctors had indicated to him that the end was near and simply advised him to enjoy his last days.

I encouraged him to come along to the healing group if he was open-minded enough and if he felt it would assist him in any manner. As with all my work I provide no guarantees, since the spirit world will always give what people need and not what they want. Peter came along to the healing group and I watched with joy as everyone sat around his body as he surrendered and lay on the floor. I have never in my life experienced so much giving. Here was

Trisha, unwell herself, wanting to help this man by giving him energy, too.

Peter surrendered himself to the spirit world that evening, releasing all the emotions of fear and anger from his body. Spirit brought many things to the surface and I remember going through those emotions with Peter. I felt for Peter, as he had received so many negative comments from the medical profession. Instead, he needed reassurance that everything would be okay, regardless of the outcome physically.

Within a couple of weeks, spirit informed me that Peter would be returning to the healing group. I was excited and informed the others. Upon starting the healing, Peter was not physically there. I felt his presence in spirit. It was a surprise to all of us. He also provided evidence of observations he had that day of Mayner in his cafe. Peter had passed over on the Monday evening and he had returned to the healing group not in the form we expected. It was a bit of a shock and it taught me so much about healing. It taught me that Peter had gained some physical healing to get him through his last days and the healing that was required was on a much higher, spiritual level. He would release his anger and fear in preparation for his new life in the spirit world and that was what he needed, not what our human side wanted.

The five usual stages of grief are denial, anger, bargaining, depression and acceptance. Not everyone experiences the stages in this linear order and some stages are much stronger for some than others. Through Peter, I learnt so much about these stages and the importance of moving through them to find peace. Grief is not only experienced by those left behind on the earth plane, it is experienced by those leaving this side of life, too. When someone is unwell, they must go through these stages of grief. The pain and hurt of going through this on their own, both mentally and spiritually, can be far greater than the physical pain of death itself. The power of spirit healing, I had realised, was on a much higher level. Peter had experienced healing at the conscious level and only when he moved into his spirit body would he have been aware of the healing at the soul level through finding peace.

Through this experience, I began to question why so much support is given on the physical side of death, such as palliative care and drug treatments for comfort, and little is provided on the spiritual side of death. If the soul were moving to the spirit world, making a transition to a new life, wouldn't it be wise to begin to discuss this new life with those who are suffering? Why is the topic avoided so much when this can't be prevented? Many people seem to believe that if you discuss death, you've given up. That's not true, for I believe we all have a contract end date here on earth. The grief stage of bargaining, in this instance, is not negotiable. If it's not negotiable, then it will happen. If it will happen, why not all share the experience together? The dying person doesn't need to go through the transition stage of physical death totally on their own on this side of life.

I find that the best way to bring up the topic is to tell wonderful stories about near-death experiences. These are documented experiences by normal, everyday people who have died and come back to tell their stories. They provide further evidence of the afterlife and the validation that our lives here on earth have a contract end date. It provides hope and understanding to those making the transition that there is life after death and nothing can ever physically harm us. There are two wonderful stories I wish to share with you. They've been in the media headlines recently and they're examples of such hope.

There was a story of a mother and child who both died during childbirth on Christmas Eve in Colorado Springs, in the United States. The doctor told the father that there was nothing that physically could be done. They even surgically opened the mother without anaesthetic when she was pronounced dead. As they pulled the baby boy from her, he was also pronounced clinically dead and together they were left in a room in preparation for the morgue. The father of the baby (after being told by doctors there was absolutely no chance at all) insisted he spend some time with the two of them before the removal of their physical bodies. As he sat on the bed beside them, both the mother and child began breathing normally again, at exactly the same time.

The mother and baby returned with no brain damage or further injuries. The doctors said they had done a thorough examination and couldn't find anything to explain why it had happened. The husband, however, provided his own explanation of the unbelievable event: *"I had everything in the world taken from me and then suddenly, everything given back to me. It was the hand of God."*[1]

There was an instance recently of a young boy who was clinically dead for more than three hours, only to return with his own explanation of heaven. The three-year-old German boy drowned on his grandfather's property, afterwards being flown by helicopter to hospital. Four doctors attempted to resuscitate him for 3 hours and 18 minutes, until his heart began beating again. Instead of the boy returning traumatised, he said he was spending time with Grandma Emmi in heaven. His grandma told him that he would go back down again quickly. The doctor's response was, *"We thought the little lad must have been brain dead but then suddenly his heart started to beat again. It was a fantastic miracle. The boy is happy and healthy. It's a wonderful thing."*[2]

People's faces light up when I tell them wonderful stories about the afterlife. Many do believe in miracles and love the thought of angelic beings taking care of us. For my mediumship events, I drive a beautiful trailer behind my car that has wonderful angel pictures on each side. I know that when the traffic is heavy and people are stressed around me on Friday afternoons, they often glance over and smile when they see my angel trailer. It's a peaceful blue colour and I know it provides them with some level of healing without ever physically meeting me. The effort of designing the trailer this way was definitely worthwhile.

I have a dear friend and work colleague, Tim, who is interested in the power of healing and assisting humanity on a larger scale. Tim and I come from very different backgrounds. Tim is a devout Catholic and I'm a dedicated medium. We really enjoy our discussions on healing as we are both part of a healing group. We laugh at the similarities of our thoughts, even though I have never read *The Bible* and Tim has never communicated with the spirit world in the way I do. We often say that working for the light is all the same, as long as the intentions are aligned with the goodness of humanity.

I'm a big believer in prayer of any kind. Prayer with the right intention to heal can send positive thoughts to a person's energy field. This in turn can move through the mental and physical energetic fields of the recipient, if they accept the healing. I believe that most religions have more in common than we think when it comes to the techniques used in prayer and healing. It doesn't matter what your beliefs, faith or religion are, you all have the ability to be healers for anyone in need as long as you send it through love and light.

A few years ago, I visited Rome and chose to take a day walk to the Vatican. The night before the tour, I had a clear vision of Mother Mary and work that was to be executed by me the next day. I trusted that I would be guided at the right time to deliver the message. It was a very hot day and I had lots of fun getting photos with nuns from all over the world in their habits. I'm not of Catholic religion but I could see the healing light in each and every one of them. They were excited to serve the greater spirit no matter what form it may have been.

The day had passed and I had totally forgotten about my visitation from Mary the night before. It was my last night in Italy, so I decided to take a late-night bus tour around Rome. I boarded the bus and took a seat and a young student priest from Norway sat beside me. There seemed to be an overwhelming sense of familiarity and I had no idea why. As the tour began, my vision began to change and I had flashes of upcoming events. I told the student priest that the bus would break down within 10 minutes and we would find ourselves in front of a hotel at exactly the same time as the rock star Madonna walked out. He looked at me and didn't say anything and I knew my vision would soon come true.

At the predicted time, the bus engine made a very loud banging sound and came to a halt. The student priest looked at me and I smiled with the anticipation of seeing Madonna. He asked how I knew and I told him Mother Mary had shown me the previous night. He told me that was unbelievable and that he had been asking her for guidance that day. He said that he came to Rome and could not decide if he wanted to be a priest or not. He then said that if she had really heard him, then Madonna would come out of the hotel as predicted by me. I had no idea that the name "Madonna" was the Italian version of the name for Mary. Within minutes, Madonna did indeed walk out of the hotel and the student priest and I looked at one another in amazement. It was great validation. We then went our separate ways since the bus tour was cancelled.

After the bus had broken down, a couple asked if I would like to join them for dinner. I accepted and we headed towards a lovely restaurant near the Vatican. Once I walked in, my radar was up and I immediately knew that I needed to speak to a husband and wife on the other side of the room. I walked up to them and said I had a message for them. I told them that Mother Mary had come to me the night before and wanted me to tell them that their daughter in England, who was extremely unwell, would be fine. To their surprise they validated this information and the husband, who had been a sceptic before, was quickly converted. They had travelled to the Vatican to pray for their daughter in the hope that Mary would hear them and provide them with answers.

I know that the spirit world sends helpers in many forms, both on this side of life and in spirit. Just like I may deliver a message to someone in need, the spirit world will send helpers to me, too, ensuring that their work can be executed in the physical world. As my audience sizes began to expand, more helpers were required in other ways. A lovely, angelic lady by the name of Lisa Jane, who has the voice of an angel, was sent to the healing group for many reasons. She's not only a kind and helping soul with a beautiful voice at platform, she also runs her own business organising events, so her input has been much appreciated. Angela is similar to Lisa Jane and helps with the administrative side of spirit work. She is fun-loving and brings a youthful side to the group. Marisia helps in many other ways with her homemade cookies and softly spoken, calming voice.

The crowds were getting bigger and I needed a new microphone system so people at the back of the room could hear me. It would cost thousands and I didn't know anyone who could assist me with that type of specialist equipment. Soon the spirit world brought forward someone to help. A man in my audience was read, with his loved ones coming through the platform and he commented afterwards that he had a friend who specialised in audio who could help me with the purchase of the system.

A couple of months later, I contacted the referred audio man and he was kind enough to provide me with a great package. One mediumship evening a while later, my microphone mouthpiece came off my headset and fell onto the floor. As I picked it up, I had a quick flash of the audio man and then just continued on with my work for the spirit world. On the Monday morning I was drawn to contact him. I attempted to call him but a different businessman answered the phone. He said that the audio man was in hospital receiving his miracle two lungs after being on a transplant list. I soon discovered that the exact day and time I received the vision on platform was the same time he went into surgery for his new lungs. I know the spirit world was informing me they were taking care of this good man, for he had indirectly provided healing to thousands of people by giving a physical voice box to loved ones in the spirit world.

[1] *Daily Telegraph, NSW, Australia, January 1, 2010.*
[2] *http://news.ninemsn.com.au/world/1037530/boy-3-met-dead-grandma-in-heaven, April 9, 2010.*

Chapter 9

When Your Time is Up

A smaller deeper step moving forward is much healthier for the soul than constant resurfacing of past old ground.
Team Spirit

In my early days of mediumship, the spirit world chose to provide me with the most valuable lesson of their teaching in terms of the processes of passing over. They were to prove to me in time that we all have a pre-defined end contract date once we have fulfilled our purpose here on earth.

It was a warm summer's evening in November and I was sitting with another medium. She handed me a photograph and asked what I could see. I don't use any tools in my mediumship, including photos, however I immediately responded to her that the lady in the photograph had late stages of stomach cancer. I could clearly see the exact date and time of her passing. I was completely surprised that this information was revealed to me – the spirit world never reveals details of when someone passes over. It serves no healing purpose as nothing can be physically done to help. But I knew they had revealed the information for greater teaching purposes.

Given that I was sitting with another medium who I totally trusted, I decided to share the information. I knew that my spirit guides had a lesson to teach us both. They revealed that the other medium must encourage this lady, who was her aunt, to resolve her anger and unfinished business with her loved ones before she crossed over into the spirit world. The medium, who confirmed that this was indeed the situation, promised to do her best to bring about some healing. The date and time were documented and I totally forgot about it – like the thousands of readings and information that come through my mind.

Around six months later, I walked into a room to meet the medium again and became very aware of a lady in spirit. She told me she was the medium's aunt and wanted to thank her for the assistance in helping her let go of her anger before crossing over. At first I was a little confused, as I had put the previous spirit communication out of my mind and had no idea what it was all about. The medium said she was waiting to see me again as her aunt had passed on the exact date and time we had documented six months earlier. The day before she passed, the medium had taken the piece of paper out and insisted that her aunt's loved ones visit her in hospital. She didn't share the information with anyone, as promised to spirit. I was completely amazed and so was she and together we'd learnt a very powerful lesson from the spirit world. When *your time's up, it's up.*

I don't think it's a coincidence that the spirit world is asking me to share this next story with you right now, in this chapter. As I'm sitting here writing this, I am now even surprised at the irony of teaching it some years later. I had totally forgotten about this story. As I'm typing, it's the exact time and date the following incident occurred, except some years later. It's pretty clever – and amazing timing – of the spirit world to bring this up, because this chapter is their teaching on the importance of timing in our lives.

Anzac Day is a remembrance day in Australia for soldiers of the Australian and New Zealand Army Corp who lost their lives in war. I always attended the dawn service with my family in Newcastle, followed by the fun of playing two-up with friends. Two-up is a gambling game enjoyed by many Australians and it's only legal to play on that particular day each year. At 9.30pm the evening before Anzac Day on that year, I was completing platform in Sydney. I was a few hours away from Newcastle and I just knew I wasn't meant to be in Newcastle for the dawn service the following morning.

I was driving home from platform that night thinking about what I would possibly be missing out on the next day. I then had a clear vision of a hamburger place I felt the need to visit. The rational side of me knew it was a bad idea – it was late at night. I never go out to eat a hamburger after platform. There was also torrential rain so I had minimal vision in front of me while driving. But I was now obsessing over hamburgers, which I don't even like! I could taste it in my mouth and the car began to smell of freshly fried chips as well. I had to go and buy these immediately, I couldn't possibly think of anything else, especially when my taste was now supplemented with full hamburger visions.

I soon turned off at the next set of lights and down the dark street towards the hamburger place and I could feel my energy field building up immensely. The hamburger place was closed but my focus was elsewhere. In the torrential rain, I was guided to turn into another street where I found an old lady lying on the side of the road in the gutter. I could clearly see a young man beside her and as I pulled up, my fear had changed to a power I had never felt before. I stepped out of the car and the young man came to confront me with anger. The lady's handbag was open on the ground. In a deep voice that even surprised me, I told him to step back and warned him that he didn't know what he was dealing with. This isn't something I would ever say or do. As he stepped back, I summoned all my strength to pick the lady up and put her in the car.

The young man ran off into the darkness. I immediately locked the doors of my car and the lady and I just sat for a moment. We were both soaking wet and I had no idea what to do. I asked her what happened and who she was. She told me she had been at work all day in her secretarial job and was on her way home to cook dinner for her husband. I found that very hard to believe, given she was in her eighties and dressed in a nightgown. She did not seem to have spent a day at work recently.

I started the car, not knowing if I needed to take the old lady to the police station or the hospital. I had no idea where she lived, since her handbag had no details in it and I felt sorry for her – she really trusted me to take her home and kept calling me an angel. In that moment of uncertainty, I was well aware of an elderly gentleman in spirit in the back of my car guiding me to her house. It was her husband indeed but he was not at home waiting for dinner as she had expected.

I drove up her driveway, walked through the wide-open back door and then helped her get ready for the night. When I left her house, I couldn't help wondering if she would be okay. My guides indicated that she would be fine and that the work required by me was done for the evening. The next morning at dawn, I could hear the Anzac service across the road and kept thinking of the old lady and why I was in Sydney and not Newcastle that year. It wasn't my time to be there that year and it was not her time to move over into the spirit world.

Before I headed up to Newcastle later that morning, I dropped in to see the old lady. She had no idea who I was and even provided a rude gesture when I knocked on the door! I was completely shocked and I knew that nothing should surprise me. She had perhaps lost all memory of the evening before and that was fine with me. She was home safe and I just needed to ensure that someone would check on her soon. I knocked on the neighbour's door and informed her about the incident the previous night. She confirmed that the woman had severe memory loss and promised she would contact her son to attend to her. The neighbour described the husband, who had passed some years earlier, which provided further validation to me of the man in spirit in the back of the car guiding me.

Many things were against the old lady that night. It was freezing cold, with torrential rain and there were trucks on the main highway with minimal vision. I have no doubt she would more than likely have died after being robbed and left in the gutter. I've never said that I have saved someone's life before – that's a strong statement. I perhaps have indirectly assisted many who wanted to cross themselves over, however on this evening I know I helped save this woman's life with the guidance of the spirit world. It validated to me further that it was not her time to go – she still had purpose on this side of life, whatever it may have been.

On another occasion as I stood in front of an audience ready to start my first reading for the evening, I couldn't help but notice the presence of Archangel Michael at the back of the room. I've had visitations from various beings over time but never have I encounted such angels while on platform. He told me clearly that I needed to speak to Petra, short for petrified. His humour was not something I expected that night. It was my first demonstration in the Central Coast region, so I didn't know if it would go down too well with a very large audience who had never seen me before.

A lady at the back of the room raised her hand and said her name was Petra. A grandmother figure who Petra hadn't known in life came through from the spirit world. I could see fire. This confirmed the Bali bombings that Petra was caught up in some years earlier. Her grandmother had also survived the bombings in the war so both their survival through these circumstances no doubt had brought their spirits together in the reading.

Many people had lost their lives the night of the Bali bombings and Petra had actively assisted those in need. On the evening of the bombings, Petra held the hand of a person who had severe trauma to the head who she believed to have been dying. There was nothing she could do for this person but to hold their hand and place a towel at the back of their head. Eventually Petra was forced to leave and save her own life. Petra carried a lot of guilt regarding this.

It was exactly 12 months later in Bali that Petra had a spiritual experience that changed her life. Whilst visiting a temple, she received an insight that appreciations of the positives in life cannot be truly felt until challenges are experienced as well. She learnt that every individual can propel themselves from a black hole and experience a happy life again and see the learning in it all. This is what enables us to become better and wiser souls.

From this experience, Petra began to have more gratitude and appreciation of life and the depression and trauma of the bombing experience began to subside for her. With the assistance of an excellent counsellor and dear friend, her life started to change. Petra's natural ability to assist souls began to extend to those greater in need. She had assisted families of the victims, but now she would formalise her talents and become a rescue officer and lifeguard. Petra is no doubt an inspiration to many people and an example that it was simply not her time. She had work to do here and she has now chosen to turn such a negative experience into a positive and healing one, especially for the many souls that will cross her path in the future.

My work colleague Trish arrived in the office one day with a photo she had taken of a magnificent sunrise shimmering from the hills. In the moment she was examining the photo on her computer, I walked into the room and we noticed an "Om" symbol in the photograph reflected over the water. The "Om" symbol is another word for God. I tuned into the photograph and asked if there was a hall nearby. Trish responded with a *yes* and soon the two of us were organising our first platform at this beautiful hall on the Central Coast.

Even from that first evening on the Central Coast, in New South Wales, I knew I was sent there for a reason. It had a wonderful community hall overlooking a beautiful wharf and water views that were breathtaking. Now, every time I drive there and park my car and trailer, I cannot help but thank Team Spirit for finding me such wonderful and peaceful premises. It has a real community sense in a lakeside environment.

The helpers on the Central Coast consist of Trish, Kath, Margaret, Christine and Debbie. I met Trish on reception at the global software company I work for and we hit it off from day one. She has seen and experienced many things in life and both she and her sister Kath have done exceptionally well, considering their tough backgrounds in New Zealand. Margaret became part of the group because she had lost a son at a young age to a brain tumour. She has a wonderful energy about her and spends so much of her day praying for others in need.

For a short period of time a lady by the name of Mary joined the group, after the suicide of her son. Team Spirit informed me that she would only be there for a little while, until she gained some healing. They were right – in no time, Mary was doing very well, finding peace again and in love once more.

When I returned to the Central Coast region after Archangel Michael's visitation, I found myself undertaking a reading with a lady in the audience regarding some healing with her mother in the spirit world. She had recovered from cancer a few times and her mother had come along in spirit to apologise for not spending more quality time with her on this side of life. She said it wasn't her time yet to come over into the spirit world and she would be beside her the whole way to ensure she maintained her physical, mental and spiritual health. The healing from the reading was moving for us all and the lady, now known to us as Christine, has become another much-needed helper recruited by my spirit guides.

There are times as a medium when you notice a living person in the audience who has a glowing aura of loving energy. On two separate evenings, a tall, attractive lady was sitting near people who were receiving readings from me and in much need of help. They had lost their children and the love from the woman towards them as they were being read was immense. I knew this wasn't a coincidence and I knew she'd been chosen by Team Spirit for some higher purpose. The name of this lady was Debbie.

Within a short period of time, the spirit world brought this lady and I together and we became immediate friends. Given that I meet thousands of people, I don't interact and become personal friends with audience members. The reason for this is that I like to remain professional and have no knowledge of people beforehand when reading them. People may think I'm being rude when I don't engage in discussion and lock myself away before an audience, however deceased loved ones and I work too hard on platform for anyone to have any doubts about integrity. It ensures that all evidence is provided by the spirit world and not by me or anyone else.

I had no real idea why Debbie had been sent to me. I was glad she offered to come on board as a helper. She brought along her sister, Kim, a couple of times to see my demonstrations, however we had not formally met. Within weeks of Debbie coming on board, Kim was unexpectedly diagnosed with cancer with only weeks to live. We were all shocked at the news and remarkably Kim took it all in her stride. She somehow accepted the brutal blow and had immense faith in the spirit world. She believed in life after death and even said that platform had more than shown her that she will continue to live on in some form or another.

When I returned home that evening after hearing the news, I realised I couldn't believe what I'd heard. How can someone in their fifties who had been feeling fit and well be given such a diagnosis and accept that it was okay? She had children and it was November and the doctors said she wouldn't even survive to spend Christmas with her family. I know I have an immense amount of faith in the spirit world, however I have never heard of anyone accepting such a short transition this way.

I began to question the phases of grief and whether or not it was just an intense bout of denial and not acceptance. The response from my guides was that she had truly accepted that her contract here on earth was ending and that she was sent to me for greater teaching purposes. What a remarkable soul. I had heard such stories but never experienced a young person coming to terms with such tragic circumstances so soon.

Debbie and her family nursed Kim around the clock, like any loving family would. That beautiful, bright angel aura I'd seen in the audience that first evening was now truly an angel preparing someone for their greatest journey. Together they discussed and laughed about the other side and made a pact to make contact when Kim arrived safely. Kim insisted in her last days that Debbie attend platform to send love and light not only to themselves but also to others in need. Debbie had a message for me that Kim had seen a vision of a man standing in a white kitchen and she had no idea why she was seeing this in her last days.

A few days later, I was standing in my kitchen in Sydney when my guides informed me that Kim had crossed over into the spirit world. They also informed me that Debbie wasn't there at the time of her passing. Those in the spirit world attended to Kim. I documented the time and waited for the news to be sent through the physical world channels.

Under these circumstances, I do not wish to be the one delivering news of someone passing over.

That afternoon, I received the formal news that Kim had indeed passed over at the time I was told by spirit. Debbie had left the house for a very short period of time and wasn't present when Kim passed over. It became clear to me that the kitchen Kim saw a few days before was my large white kitchen in Sydney and the man was one of the men I believe to be my spirit guides. Kim hadn't seen my kitchen before and now I know she was meant to tell Debbie and me as part of her validation of crossing over and arriving okay in the spirit world. The arrival was so pre-ordained in that moment it was given to us all for teaching purposes a few days earlier.

Kim had provided another level of teaching in my mediumship. Through thousands of readings, I knew from the spirits that so much of our lives, including our endings, are pre-ordained. But Kim had provided a higher-level comfort in accepting when our time is up. She knew that her spirit could not die and she knew that the physical body is only a temporary vehicle for a temporary experience. The soul lives on forever and she will carry on her memories in her consciousness, even though her physical time here on earth is now completed.

Chapter 10

High-flying Fiona

You are never alone. Loneliness is only for those who believe nothing else exists outside ourselves.
Team Spirit

As I boarded the plane for England, I was excited to start a six-week journey that would involve a combination of work, mediumship and holiday. Life couldn't have been better and as the plane flew high into the sky, I started to relax in my own company again.

One morning before preparing to go into the office for work in England, I decided to go downstairs into the hotel gymnasium as I'd had problems sleeping after the long trip. When I started my exercises, I became very aware of Eunice. She passed into the spirit world around three years earlier as a result of a combination of lung cancer and emphysema. She made her presence known to me but didn't discuss why she had come to visit.

Eunice is the mother of my brother-in-law Shane. I have stayed with Therese and Shane on weekends for many years when I travel up the coast to visit my family, so he's more of a brother to me than a brother-in-law. If anyone knows how twins operate, they will understand that when you marry one of them, the other one seems to come along as part of the package. Shane has never minded this and we have a great understanding and respect for one another on many levels.

Once I called Therese back in Australia, she informed me that some terrible news had arrived that day. Fiona, Shane's sister from Melbourne had been diagnosed with stage four terminal bile duct cancer. The doctors had limited treatment and options. This left Fiona and everyone else in a shattered state of mind. Fiona was informed of the news on her mother Eunice's birthday, which explained the brief visitation from her in spirit.

As I travelled across the United Kingdom after completing my work, I was in a state of disbelief about the news. I was halfway around the world, about to start two weeks of mediumship with the spirit world, and none of this information was given to me. Why had Team Spirit not shared this with me? I understood the universal laws of mediumship – that certain information can't be revealed without a purpose – but the human part of me still wondered.

Fiona was 47 years of age, extremely fit and did not smoke or drink. The bile duct cancer was also in her liver. She was a vegetarian, ate healthily and wouldn't harm a fly. She had many beef cows on her property that she named personally with the intention of them being more pets than anything else. With her flaming red hair and freckly face, her wit and humour could easily outsmart anyone who crossed her path.

To say that Fiona was a high achiever would be an understatement. She was a managing director of an information technology consultancy company and was seen in the financial sections of Australia's leading newspapers for her achievements. She worked hard all her life and was never ashamed to admit that she'd been brought up in a working class suburb in Newcastle, Australia. She won medals at university for weightlifting and hockey. There was no women's hockey team at the time, so she simply joined the men's team as a solution to her problem.

Fiona never took no for an answer – anything and everything was possible – so when she was confronted with her illness, there was one thing of which she was certain. She would fight it all the way. She never sought the approval of doctors or anyone else and she maintained her positive spirit. She believed in the power of the mind and she was a prime example of how her positive thoughts had made her a success in life. She was open to anything that was positive and it was this mindset that bonded the two of us together at a much deeper level.

When I arrived for my second part of the trip to commence mediumship in England, I met another medium on the first day who was in exactly the same circumstances as me. It was a comfort to know that I wasn't on my own and together we discussed our situations. She told me her friend being unwell was one of the toughest lessons she had to go through and we agreed we needed to trust in the greater plan regarding the higher purpose of everyone's contract in life. She reminded me that we are just the instruments of this work and sometimes the instrument does not always play the tune we like to hear.

Over the next two weeks of solid mediumship, I sent positive thoughts to Fiona and let her know that I would be with her all the way, through mind, body and spirit. She would not need to go through this alone – we were there for her no matter how tough things may become. Being among the energies of the spirit world was the best place for me to be and especially with another medium who understood the circumstances.

Once I completed my overseas trip, I returned to Australia and spent some time with Fiona on the phone. Her first question was whether or not she would get through this terrible illness. Fiona was in the prime of her life. She was in love with her partner Ralf and in the middle of building a very big home on her property. She had begun to think of an early retirement working on the land. Her illness was certainly not what she was expecting, so there needed to be some adjustments in her mindset for her to comprehend that she was actually very physically ill.

I reassured her that although I didn't have all the answers, I guaranteed and promised from day one that I would walk the journey with her all the way, wherever it may take us. I explained to her that we all have contracts and this learning is our learning and together we must see it as a conglomerate path for all involved. This experience was chosen for a reason at a much higher soul level and I trusted in this.

Every morning before work, I would call Fiona and we'd chat on the phone. She'd been part of the family for 17 years but we learnt more about each other's lives in that first month than we did in all those years. Every day, I would ask her what she was afraid of and together we talked about it as a shared issue. I would give her my perspective on things and then ask how she felt about the situation. Just by talking with me, she answered most of her own questions out loud and that provided her with enough peace and comfort for another day.

We would often laugh at the similarities of our own lives. The two of us had attended the same university, where we both ended up working, and then later on in life worked on exactly the same computer product for some years. Both of us worked in major Australian cities during the week and loved returning to larger properties with livestock on the weekends. In all this, we never really crossed paths on professional or personal levels. I would only see Fiona at major family functions, as she lived some 12 hours away from Shane and Therese. We had so much catching up to do and somehow the discussions about the illness would fade away into the background.

Given that Fiona was so far away physically, spirit guided me to an alternative healer who could provide comfort to her on a physical and spiritual level. She lived locally, in the same country town as Fiona and her name was Tanja. They bonded immediately – Tanja shared the same positivity and enthusiasm for life as both Fiona and I. Tanja would provide counselling, massage and alternative therapies to Fiona, including meditation. I felt much more at ease when I knew someone spiritual was on the physical ground force with Fiona as well.

Over the next few months, Fiona's illness worsened and she had to have regular stomach draining on Wednesday mornings to give her a bit of comfort. Today, almost a year later, I still think of those Wednesdays and our phone calls. When I was in Melbourne visiting, I attended the hospital sessions with Fiona and the pain she endured without any drugs was unbelievable. Fiona refused to have any type of drug in her body, including painkillers, even when doctors created new holes in her stomach for the tubing.

It was a warm, early January morning in Sydney when I found myself almost running through the door of my unit with disbelief. I had just had a clear vision of Fiona's soul speaking to me. She told me that my work was to assist her through the light and she smiled as she let go of my hand and walked through a tunnel of light. I saw flashes of events in front of me and suddenly the vision was gone. I knew that Fiona had not passed over – she was not in the spirit form I normally see – and the last time we spoke she was doing fine. It was her soul, at another level, speaking to me and I had never in my life experienced such a situation from a living person on this side of life.

That morning I couldn't go back to sleep, so I decided to walk down to the beach. I tried to block what I'd seen from my mind and was soon prompted by my team of spirit guides of the real visitation and learning yet to come. Fiona and I had an agreement in this life and she came to tell me the importance of this to heal many others. Even though a part of me felt so much love as she let go of my hand and smiled, I missed her already. I didn't want to know any more information. There was nothing I could do to change the situation and every part of me knew there was greater teaching involved.

As the months progressed, our conversations became very spiritual and I shared everything with her about my mediumship. She was interested in all the details and believed in so much of my work, even though she had physically not seen it all in action. We had a soul connection. We loved one another like sisters – I took the morning-shift phone calls, Therese chatted with her at night and together the three of us were all connected. We were not connected by Fiona's illness but with a level of understanding that nothing could separate us no matter what. It is only when we feel isolated and separated that we feel alone. Our life experiences are not our own, they are to be shared with each and every person around us. From these experiences we all grow and evolve into the souls we are today.

Fiona decided to send her close friend and work colleague, Jackie, to one of my platform events in Sydney. When I met Jackie afterwards, I could see another version of Fiona in so many ways. They both had a cheeky laugh that matched their high levels of intelligence and they were always striving for the next challenge in life. Jackie and I immediately became friends and we stayed in contact as Fiona's health deteriorated.

One day, Jackie had enough of the company she was working for and decided to resign and travel to Melbourne to be with Fiona. This was out of character for Jackie as she was hardworking and always tried to do the best for everyone around her, including her family. But something had changed. Jackie was the one who had taken Fiona to her own doctor for the original tests and it seemed that the experience of it all was now driving some of Jackie's life-changing decisions. Together the two of them laughed and enjoyed each other's company and I know this meant a lot to Fiona at the time.

Once Jackie had left the property, I started to feel an urge that it was time for us to visit again. I booked flights for Therese, Shane and I to go to Melbourne the following day. I clearly remember the song, *Send Me an Angel*, on the radio when we were driving into the property. Everything now seemed familiar to me on a deeper level and I couldn't work out what it was. As we arrived at the house and greeted Fiona, her face lit up like a Christmas tree. We were together again and nothing could separate us.

For the next 24 hours we lay beside her in bed, told stories and laughed. A car drove up the driveway to deliver flowers from her work. I could now understand the familiarity. In my vision six months earlier, there were flashes of events before my eyes. Fiona stepped into the light and these events were unfolding in front of me right now, hour by hour. Tanja arrived unexpectedly that afternoon and together we lit a candle in the bedroom at sunset and phoned Jackie to include her as well. Glenda, Fiona's carer and best friend, was also there.

We all laughed and Fiona smiled at us in a way I hadn't seen for a very long time. She had found peace and I understood the love I felt in the vision that morning. She was ready and as she went in and out of consciousness in the later hours, out of nowhere she tightly squeezed my hand and smiled at me as I lay beside her. We had wrapped her in a beautiful pink blanket that Jackie had bought for her, so everyone was with her that night. With her last energy, she crossed her fingers. As she let go of my hand, it was the last time I consciously spoke to Fiona in physical form. She passed away peacefully the next morning, only a couple of hours before we were due to fly back to Newcastle. Fiona was now at peace and with her mother, Eunice. Her physical world struggles were over.

I had no idea Fiona would go that fast. I had no idea of the timing at all until I arrived at the property and the sequence of events in my vision began to unfold. Glenda did much more for Fiona than any best friend could ever do for someone. She was Fiona's personal assistant for many years and had taken onboard the duties of a carer. This helped Ralf immensely as I can't imagine how hard it would have been for him to care for her by himself.

Fiona spent a lot of her time flying for work, so I found it ironic that we flew in, she passed away and then we flew out again. Her soul would have carefully chosen this grand exit and she would not have had it any other way.

She had passed away on Ralf's birthday and their anniversary, as well as the anniversary of my own grandmother's funeral. I acknowledged the significance of this in my own life contract and the greater teaching of it all. Grandma and Fiona were two powerful women with unforgettable teaching not only to me but also to the thousands who will heal through their stories. I believe that death is only tragic when you see no greater purpose in it. Fiona's experience was also my experience and from this both our souls have evolved to another level.

The vision that earlier January morning was Fiona's soul, her higher self, that part of our spirit that acknowledges this whole earthly experience and its purpose. Some may think the vision would be haunting but I see it only as a privilege. A privilege that her higher soul thought I was ready to accept the information at the lower human soul level and learn from it; a privilege that she chose me to be part of her life contract and to provide healing to you all through her own life experience. That is high-flying Fiona and she continues to guide many of us today from the other side of life in spirit.

Chapter 11

Knowing Me, Knowing You

Magic moments shouldn't only be recognised when they disappear.
Team Spirit

Perhaps one of the greatest misconceptions about mediums is that we have a constant direct phone line to the spirit world and we can contact them whenever we need something or wish to speak to our loved ones who have passed over. This is far from the truth. The gift of mediumship is used for serving others and not for self-servicing. The spirit world would not want to work with someone who has the intention of using mediumship for their own needs – they simply would not answer the phone. I believe it's a privilege and not a right and I think it's important to educate on the difference.

I believe that my two close friends, Tracey and Lina, were chosen in this life for a reason. They have never asked me for a reading and they have never judged me for any of the work I do. They are truly blessings in disguise and I am so fortunate to call them my good mates. I could not have asked for better companions throughout the years, even throughout the growth of my mediumship path.

With me, they have remained grounded in it all and treat me as Louise their friend and not a medium. This has made our friendship grow even stronger over time.

Lina was extremely close to her grandmother and a period of time after her grandmother's passing, her spirit made herself known to me. The visitation was not just to drop in and say hello. It served a greater purpose. She had a direct message for Lina's sister Julie to look after herself and her husband. She provided evidence of her observations from the spirit world. I had no idea beforehand of the detailed information she provided in the reading.

Tracey lost her mother, Jan, a few years ago suddenly to heart failure. Her presence was around me on special occasions, such as weddings and birthdays, and one day she really manifested herself to me. I was driving on the highway to Newcastle, where Tracey lives, and suddenly there was Jan sitting right next to me in the car. She told me that Tracey was pregnant. Even though the news surprised me, I asked her to provide specific information of another incident she had observed so I could pass on some strong evidence of her visitation to Tracey.

The minute I arrived in Newcastle, I called Tracey and she confirmed that she was indeed pregnant. She hadn't shared the information with anyone else and an incident her mother described in the lounge room the day before was exactly what happened. I was happy for Tracey that she was pregnant and she was happy that her mum was in the wings ready to assist her in bringing the unborn child into the physical world. Up until that day, her mother hadn't come through strongly. That particular day she came as a result of Tracey needing her mother, so from this need came a greater purpose in the visitation.

It's much harder to read for someone you know than someone you don't know. People think it would be easier to read friends but that's not the case at all. If you know someone, their loved ones are very limited in what they can give you as evidence, as they must eliminate all possible thoughts that are in the medium's mind beforehand. I believe they scan my mind to see what I already know first and this would take a lot of energy. Once this has been done, they then know what they can give as new information or evidence of survival.

Fortunately, I have read for very few people in the audiences who I know, which is great. A part of me hesitates to read for them, even though I have no choice, as I know how tough the job is for both their loved ones in the spirit world and me. I had an incident with my friend Margot, who attended platform with my flatmate Sonja. Her grandfather came through from the spirit world. I knew nothing of Margot's background at this time, as we had just met briefly on a few occasions. Apart from the usual names and incidents I couldn't have known, he wanted her mother to know that the angels were drawing close to her as part of his healing message. He also mentioned problems with her hips and walking. It was not long after this reading that Margot's mother, Lola, passed unexpectedly into the spirit world. Lola indicated the night before her passing that her hips were hurting and aching. This reading later provided Margot with comfort and understanding that her grandfather was preparing both her and her mother for transition, even though that was not directly revealed in the reading that night.

A very funny incident occurred on platform one evening that had me in laughter afterwards at the desperation of the spirit world to grab my attention. My two close friends in Sydney, Simone and a second friend called Fiona, have always supported me in my mediumship. They introduced me to another friend a couple of years ago, Yasmin, and the three of us would often go out together. I didn't know anything about Yasmin's background at all since we often just spoke about current life experiences and enjoyed the general chatter of good friends.

One evening, Yasmin decided to attend platform with a friend I hadn't met. Simone and Fiona weren't there, which was a relief as I could just imagine them laughing over the whole incident. Yasmin was sitting in the front row when, just before I was about to start the first reading, a man in spirit got my attention on platform. The man had the loudest voice I'd ever heard and he told me his name was Uncle Bill.

I began to relay information to the audience, including the name of a father and mother figure and details of a wedding many years ago in which Uncle Bill gave the person away. I described this real character in detail and there was silence. As I waited for someone to own this man in spirit, he kept laughing and dancing on the platform like I had never seen before. I relayed his personality to the audience and now everyone was laughing. To my surprise, Yasmin raised her hand and claimed good old Uncle Bill.

I had no idea of Yasmin's background or history, so the reading was interesting for me, too, especially with such a vibrant spirit. He provided more than excellent evidence, including names and information I could possibly not have known. As Yasmin's mum was not physically well, he wanted to let her know he was around. The reading provided Yasmin with a great amount of healing, and her mother as well as she relayed the message from spirit. A few months later, Yasmin's mum Patricia passed into the spirit world and into the awaiting arms of Uncle Bill.

If you're a friend of mine reading this book, don't be worried that if you're chosen for a reading, someone will pass over soon or you'll fall pregnant! That's not the case in most of my readings. The purpose of mediumship is to provide healing. These stories were simply chosen to explain the importance of the need for healing by the spirit world, even amongst people who are considered my friends. Margot and Yasmin, like everyone else, had a need that evening with spirit and it's this need that determines my work on platform. I had no idea, like them, that their loved ones would be passing over until it happened. But afterwards, we could all see the beauty in the messages. Sometimes spirit indirectly prepares us in their own way for those about to pass over, or even those coming in from the spirit world, like in the case of Tracey's pregnancy. It's this wonder, the power of love in clearing the way for life between the two worlds, that makes all this work worthwhile.

Sometimes the humour and healing in mediumship doesn't stop after the messages have been passed on by the spirit world. I attended the christening of Tracey's baby in a local Catholic church. It was a lovely service by a great priest and when the time came to pour the water on the baby's head, the priest said loudly to the baby boy: *"You will not dabble with the occult."* The word *occult* seems frightening but it simply means to be hidden from the eye or the understanding. At this stage, some people were looking at me and I could see the irony of it all. Tracey's mum was a dedicated Catholic and also used the services of a medium once she passed over. She could see the truth in our work and the grandson she told me about was now sitting right in front of me in physical form. I don't take things personally as I know that one day we will all cross over into the spirit world and many who would not have used my services on this side of physical life certainly will once they see the truth and healing in it from the other side.

After I walked into the church at Yasmin's mother's funeral, I found myself sitting next to a lady who seemed to be very glad to see me. I didn't recognise her but she was keen to share the sheet music with me. She went on to explain that she had attended one of my audience sessions many months earlier and her loved ones from the spirit world gave great evidence and healing to her. Now the priest was only metres away, wondering what this woman was talking about. I wasn't being rude and I had no recollection at all since I see thousands of people and conduct hundreds of readings. I also felt it was not the time and place to discuss mediumship as it was Yasmin's mum's celebration of life that day.

I continued to sit with this lovely lady and she was still intrigued – she wondered if people from the spirit world were present at the funeral. I didn't discuss what I was seeing and just went within myself and started to tune out the spirit people in the room who had arrived for the grand party. Uncle Bill was one of them and I'm sure that if he had my attention for too long, I wouldn't be focusing on the physical world funeral service. Another lady across the room, who had also been read in an audience in another region, recognised me as well.

Here I was at a funeral service and people were fascinated by what was going on with the medium and not the priest. The medium had provided them with evidence of the afterlife and proof of survival beforehand, so they were looking to me to provide them with insights of what was actually going on in the room. Of course, I didn't make eye contact and I kept to myself. It was interesting seeing things from another perspective. People want to know what happens when you die: *Where was Patricia? Was she there at her own service?* These are questions that are not answered at funeral services.

To answer these questions in short, yes, spirits attend their own funerals. I have seen this in many readings when specific details have been brought through, including what they were wearing in the coffin, words written on notes and even the exact cost of the funeral. On rare occasions, if the spirits have come through within a week of passing, they have asked for parts of their own service to be changed. On some occasions, funeral directors have attended my demonstrations. I know they must feel the presence of spirits when preparing their bodies.

Funerals play an important part in your loved ones' healing as well. The spirit world would prefer they have a service to celebrate life, since they have started a new life once completing physical death.

The physical body is like a very wet, heavy coat once it's disposed of; they're free to move around with a body that replicates their physical body when it was in their prime. A funeral is a celebration of new life in the spirit world and so if some of this can be incorporated into the funeral service that would help the spirits in their transition.

When I stood up at High-flying Fiona's funeral, the priest said: *"Louise will now be doing a reading."* This, of course, involved reading a poem. However, what if it was a mediumship reading? What would Fiona say about herself? She did live a remarkable life but would she also mention her regrets and bad points in life? These details always seem to be left out of funeral services and I think they would inspire others to live life to the full. Perhaps people would attempt to achieve more of their dreams if the spirit coming through said you could never ever fail. Now that would be inspirational!

High-flying Fiona more than demonstrated her inspiration some months after she passed with an amazing incident that even surprised me. Due to the thousands of requests for individual readings, I place them all in a barrel and only those that are drawn out have the opportunity to sit with me in my home for a one-on-one reading. The odds are very small and at this stage, it's the fairest way I can deliver my individual reading work for the spirit world.

One day, I placed my hand in the barrel to schedule my once-a-month reading day. The name I pulled from the barrel was a man by the name of Peter. To my surprise, it was Fiona's ex-husband. He had attended a platform event the year before Fiona even passed. Now he would be coming for a sitting and it was the first time anyone I had known was pulled from the barrel. I was excited at the possibility of what this could teach me. Like Yasmin and Margot, there needed to be a greater purpose of healing.

Peter lived a long distance away and he agreed to travel to attend the reading. I had only met Peter a couple of times as he spent most of his time overseas and I have little knowledge of his background. He has an education in psychology and I knew he would be a great challenge for the reading. I was hoping that High-flying Fiona was up for it, too, and together we could provide not only healing for Peter but also make a difference in the assessment of the mechanics of mediumship.

Peter arrived for the reading and without hesitation his father came forward, followed by Fiona. I realised in that moment how much I had missed her. I had seen her in spirit a number of times but this time we had an official appointment. The spirit world know how strict I am on my barrel system so they used it to not only teach me something but to provide me with healing as well. There was a part of me that needed healing, too, and together we blended our energy and off we went into the reading.

It was the old Fiona coming through with flying colours. She was not unwell and she didn't need a break. She was vibrant, witty and ready for the challenge. The challenge was definitely there – reading for someone I knew meant very specific evidence was required. She gave very private information and events about Peter I couldn't have possibly known or obtained from anyone else. She also included the unique name of his close friend Neilson from many years earlier.

For an hour, the two of us gave Peter all we had and it left the three of us feeling the joy and power of mediumship. The reading was only six months after Fiona had passed and she was doing well due to all the spiritual healing she had received beforehand. As she disconnected her energy and sent all her love, I realised I'd received a taste of my own healing medicine. Mediumship provides healing to all, including the medium at times. We often ask who massages the masseuse and the same applies to mediumship. The spirit world never ceases to amaze me, whether they are knowing me or knowing you.

Chapter 12

The Myths of Murders and Suicides

If you feel your life at times may be in hot water, covering it up may only cause it to eventually boil over.
Team Spirit

I am very fortunate that the spirit world has trusted me with some of the most delicate areas of healing through mediumship. As I begin this chapter, I already know that some of you will need to open your mind to other explanations and possibilities for those passing through murder and suicide. So much negativity has been placed around these types of deaths that I hope this chapter provides you with some further insights and perhaps you will then view them differently, through the eyes of the spirits.

I was in my early twenties when I received a distressed phone call that my friend Rachel had passed of suicide. She was only young, thirty years of age and she had her whole life ahead of her. I could only imagine how painful life must have been for Rachel in the end. I had known both her sisters, Jill and Goldie, for some years.

A few years later, Rachel made herself known to me while I was reading for someone else. She was standing tall and very attractive in a beautiful floral dress. Her olive skin and big, deep eyes didn't show the stresses of the earth plane and the hormonal imbalances that were brought about through postnatal depression. She was vibrant and I was happy to invite her in to teach me healing in her own way. She was always quiet in personality and we had an understanding between us that enabled our energy to blend well together.

Through Rachel, I learnt that some souls find their experiences here on earth too harsh. Their personalities are not able to understand life here and they can feel that they wish to go home. I know they're not conscious of this home at the time and they feel there's a more peaceful place for their soul. I believe that their higher self, that part of us in spirit, disconnects with the human lower ego. This disconnection then ultimately leads them to take their own lives.

We are all comprised of the human ego and the human spirit. The ego is what grounds us here to the material world in order for us to have a physical life experience. The spirit, however, is that higher part of us that drives the experience here on earth to achieve a certain purpose and understanding of life. Ideally, a balance between the two is required in order to live a sustainable life without the consequences of self-destruction or self over-empowerment.

The best way to describe the human ego and spirit is through the legendary story, *The Two Wolves*. One evening a Cherokee told his grandson about a battle that goes on inside people. He said, "My son, the battle is between two wolves inside us all. One is the darker of the wolves. It is anger, envy, jealousy, sorrow, regret, greed, arrogance, self-pity, guilt, resentment, inferiority, lies, false pride, superiority and, ultimately, all parts of the human ego. The other wolf is light. It provides joy, peace, hope, serenity, humility, kindness, benevolence, empathy, generosity, truth, compassion and love, all of which are represented by the human spirit." The grandson asked, "If there's a constant battle between the human ego and spirit, then which wolf wins?" The old Cherokee simply replied, "The one you choose to feed."

I believe that if every soul read *The Two Wolves* and lived its truth each and every day, then peace here on earth could be restored. We are all souls living amongst a community of other souls and our own energy is very much affected by the energy of those around us. The human spirit has an understanding that we are all connected, all part of the same source. The less we're connected to our spirit through anger, fear and resentment, the less we have an understanding that we are all equal and powerful, loving beings.

If we no longer connect to our own higher spirit, it's difficult to connect with those around us. It's this disconnection to our own spirit and the spirits of those around us that allows the human ego, through lack of self-love, to make a decision to exit. Life has been given to us all through free will and so divine intervention is not permitted to break that universal law that was so rightly given to each and every soul at physical birth. Every soul has the right to make their own choices in life, whether or not we judge those decisions to be good or bad.

So does this pain end once someone decides to voluntarily exit this earthly experience? The physical pain will end but the person will still need to go through some level of soul healing in the spirit world. Whatever their spirit could not face here on earth, they will still need to work through it on the other side. A decision to exit doesn't mean they're free of all the learning that the souls left behind on earth are going through. They'll be well aware of the pain that has been caused, with some of them regretting the experience for a while, whereas others may quickly move forward in the hope of using their experience to heal others. I know Rachel has been sent to me for this purpose, as she has assisted me on so many occasions in bringing forward those who have passed in this manner. Either way, this healing is done in a very loving and compassionate environment, with no punishment whatsoever.

There was a period in my platforms when spirits who had worked as priests here on earth were coming through for readings. These priests were from a variety of religions and this fascinated me. A couple of them even had connections with the Vatican in their physical life. After a priest would come through, someone else who had passed from suicide would then come through the platform in the next reading. The spirit world provided no explanation of this pattern for some months, until one day they gave me an insight I least expected.

My team of spirit guides explained the greater purpose of their teaching and the new learning that must be brought here on earth. They stated that priests are just like everyone else and they, too, can require immense amounts of healing once they pass over into the spirit world, due to their lack of understanding of healing taught traditionally here on earth.

Here's an example of the immense healing that may be required by a priest once they pass over into the spirit world. If a priest had addressed around 50,000 people in their lifetime and around 500 of those souls decided to take their own lives, these souls may have been told that if they committed suicide they would end up in a place called hell. So when those 500 souls did undertake that act in a confused state, they would have died believing that after death they would be judged and sent to that dark place.

Healing guides and loved ones will attempt to reach out and provide help to those souls who have taken their own lives. If they had strong religious beliefs here on earth, they may want to be left alone and not trust their loved ones reaching out in the spirit world. They may then believe they will be judged and sent for punishment. Once a priest crosses over and sees that their work has caused further pain rather than healing to others, they will want to assist as they now live in a world of truth and knowingness of connectivity. However, the healing guides will advise them that it's not a good idea to reach out as the priest had told them in life that the devil disguises itself. A confused soul may really believe they're on their way to hell if the priest attempts to work with them.

The solution to this is to allow the medium to work with the spirits to let go of their strong religious beliefs and seek healing from souls without judgement and punishment. The priest now sees in the world of light and truth that the medium, who they previously considered to be linked to the devil, is now cleaning up the problems created by strong human ego beliefs. Not only do mediums work for the light, they are constantly putting up with the negative comments from some religious groups when they are on this side of life. It is this awareness once crossing over that encourages the priests to come back through the platform and tell the truth. It is this speaking of truth that provides healing not only to the priests in spirit but also to those who have strong religious beliefs on both sides of life and to those who fear that their loved ones are in such a dark place.

The example above is not common among all priests as I know there are many who are open to the work of mediumship and who do not attempt to separate themselves through superiority. These priests are of light and through connectivity they would never have any soul believe they are worthless and in need of punishment. Separation or disconnection as seen by the story *The Two Wolves* is the first sign of the human ego. Anyone who believes their beliefs are more superior to and more right than others is not working from the greater spirit of humanity – it's the human ego speaking. Further to this, if the darker wolf of fear is used to promote such beliefs, then you need to question which wolf you decide to feed. Each and every soul has the right to an eternal and peaceful life no matter what his or her own circumstances may be.

One evening, my guides explained to me the rationality behind the devil and a place called hell. Only recently, thank God, the former pope publicly admitted there is no such place [1]. My guides said that the word "devil" was derived from simply taking the word "lived" and spelling it backwards. The word "evil" is much the same, as it is simply "live" when spelt backwards. If we indulge in the physical world temptations of the human ego or sins such as pride, envy, anger, sloth, greed, gluttony and lust, then we are indulging in the human needs of life and not of our spirit.

There was original truth in these thoughts and then it was decided to create a character for the human ego outside of the self so it could easily be identified. Human beings lack great levels of discipline so it would be better if someone else could control our temptations and therefore enforce punishment at will. If the devil does actually exist, then why have there been no sightings or photographs such as those of Mother Mary and Jesus, who actually did live and provide healing and truth to the masses?

From a scientific point of view, it would be impossible for a soul to move to a vibration lower than earth (hell). As explained in a previous chapter, *Mechanics of Mediumship*, the physical world is a world of matter that vibrates at a lower frequency than the spirit world. Everything exists here on earth through the formation of atoms that bond together due to the slowness of the frequency of energy. When someone dies and dematerialises, they are no longer of matter and their spirit body then vibrates at a much higher frequency in another world.

This is why all the spirit world can see us, since our frequency is lower than theirs. If there was life below our own frequency here on earth (hell), we should all see and experience it as well, since the matter would be much denser due to the slower vibrational frequency. How can someone who has taken their own life, who no longer has a physical body, move into a world (hell) that's much denser than when they had a physical body? It is scientifically impossible and would defy all the universal laws of energy. Through hundreds of readings of suicides, I know them to be in exactly the same place as everyone else in the spirit world.

The earth plane is full of so many different souls and characters. There are people walking around committing crimes, saving lives, suffering from depression and spreading the word of light. The same also applies to the spirit world. There are many walks of life but no crime or hatred, only love and truth. Whether or not you have taken your life, you will end up in the same place as everyone else, despite your mindset being confused and requiring healing.

We are all of spirit and even though there may be differing levels of awareness in the spirit world, just like on earth, everyone is entitled to healing and love and no soul is ever punished or judged by a higher force. Souls do enough of that to themselves once they see all truth. If they feel the need to reflect and heal from their circumstances, then they will do so. Through the power of mediumship, an immense amount of healing can be obtained from both sides of life.

One of the most powerful readings of suicide was from a man in spirit by the name of Alan, who came through identifying himself clearly with names, locations and events. Alan was highly intelligent and in his late twenties. After completing his doctorate in engineering and suffering a long battle with schizophrenia, he took his life by jumping from a high-rise building. His wife, sitting in the back row of the audience, was totally surprised and raised her hand to claim him to be her husband.

Alan referred to his wife as a violin – her name was Viola and she did in fact play the violin. He had left behind a small baby and had watched the child grow from the spirit world over the years. Alan was now doing well after a period of healing and wanted his wife to know that one day they would meet again in the spirit world, as she was the love of his life. Despite the circumstances, Viola has lived a happy and productive life for the past 20 years and no doubt is an inspiration to many. The timing of the reading was incredible as Alan's good friend's wife, who Viola had met through work only recently, was also in the audience. Viola had also not seen Alan's good friend since the day of the funeral 20 years ago and they were meeting again for the first time the same day of this reading. The reading has further inspired Viola to perhaps one day put pen to paper and share with the world the truth of mental health issues.

Living with police over the years was no doubt my training ground regarding learning the mechanics of crime and the thought processes that both a victim and perpetrator must go through under such circumstances. I know I have experienced a lot of connections with murder throughout my platforms and individual readings – more than the average medium. But due to the risk from these perpetrators still living today, I will not discuss any of those crimes at length in this book. I will, however, discuss one of these readings in this chapter since both the victim and perpetrator are now in the spirit world. The daughter of the family has also given permission for me to share this with you and I am honoured she has allowed this in order to teach you some of the myths around murders.

It was a normal platform evening with an audience in Sydney and I could feel myself getting a little more nervous than usual beforehand. I normally don't get too nervous before an event as I spend around 10 minutes of quiet time surrendering to my team in the spirit world. As I walked out to the audience, I completed the first reading and then started to feel more quiet than usual. I noticed a lady standing on my platform holding a shotgun and to my surprise I had no words. I asked this lady to clearly identify herself, which she did, and then she began to relay the events of a murder she was involved in. I soon realised that the woman was not the victim but rather the perpetrator of the crime.

Immediately, I became aware of a gentleman in spirit standing to the left of me and he was the victim of this crime. Never before had I dealt with both sides of the story publicly on a platform. His name was Eric and he had been shot and killed by Violet, his wife, with the assistance of her son. I could see that the lady had been through a lot of abuse from this man throughout her life. As she was telling me her story, he was agreeing with what she said about the abuse she had endured from him before the murder. I couldn't believe what I was seeing and hearing. Here was a situation of two people in a world of truth now telling the story how it was. There seemed to be a level of agreement that unfortunately did not occur here in the physical world.

After suffering years of mental and physical abuse, Violet and her son had finally taken action and were jailed for murder. She had suffered enough and so had Eric and now it was time for them both to come forward and share their experience and learning with the audience. In a world of truth, the two of them were reunited and forced to face any unfinished healing that may have been experienced here on earth. They were no longer confined to the thoughts of the human ego body. They were now in spirit where the soul does not know hatred and resentment like it exists on this side of life. The soul has survived many lives and, like the previous incarnated one, it will work through any unfinished healing like all souls do.

It's not a coincidence that both the names Viola and Violet have been used in this chapter by the spirit world. Both these souls have blossomed like flowers through experiences that most human souls would never wish to endure. Both of them would have faced immense judgements because of their circumstances and they have now chosen on both sides of life to attempt to educate others on forgiveness and healing. No experience, whether you view it as dark or light is ever wasted. It is only when we see no greater purpose in the teaching of that experience that the loss is truly tragic.

I have had many situations where a victim has come through and quickly moved past the details of a brutal murder. The family here may still feel hatred towards the perpetrator and I know that one day the victim and perpetrator will need to face one another and heal. The victim may have already been through healing and the final part of healing may occur when the perpetrator has crossed over. This facing of souls to one another is not done by the judgement of a higher force. A greater judgement will occur and that's through self-reflection of truth in the afterlife.

While living here on earth, the perpetrator doesn't have the ability to see this truth, as they are caught up in the human ego mind of anger, fear, frustration and perhaps even guilt. This is why I never place myself at any risk with a perpetrator, as you're dealing with a soul who has been driven by ego thoughts, whether or not this was out of protection or fear, like Violet, or simply selfish temptations to meet their own ego needs.

When released from the human body through eventual physical death they will see all truth in the spirit world. Each and every soul through a life review will experience not only all the pain and suffering they have personally experienced in their own lives but also any pain they have placed on others here on earth. This connectivity that occurs at the soul level through a life review in the spirit world is extremely powerful and only then can most of these souls feel any true remorse for their own actions. All these souls end up in the same place even though their awareness may vibrate at different frequencies depending on their own self-love and love for others.

Once a soul experiences the suffering they may have caused, they may come back through a medium to provide healing for those involved. They may also decide to return to the earth plane to experience this pain themselves personally in another life through the universal laws of cause and effect, or karma, as you may know it. Either way, we're not in the position to place judgement, as this is a contractual agreement for those souls involved. We do not know the history of past lives or karmic debt that may have been incurred previously, or what greater plan of learning has been set up by divine order.

Only those souls involved can do the forgiving with one another. As the medium, I don't have the power to do this and neither do any of the loved ones that are left behind. It's no different to disputes that occur here on earth, except in the spirit world all truth is revealed and there's no place to hide. If someone who has experienced pain in this life crosses over and has forgiven those involved, I respect this greatly as it indicates they are more advanced souls who understand that we are all part of the same source, evolving through life experiences, including pain. They understand the connectivity of the source and from this truth they have moved on with a new life in the spirit world through healing, love and compassion for both themselves as well as others.

[1]

http://www.vatican.va/holy_father/john_paul_ii/audiences/1999/documents/hf_jp-ii_aud_28071999_en.html

Vatican Weekly Address, July 28, 1999
POPE JOHN PAUL II REJECTS REALITY OF A LITERAL HELL

The images of hell that Sacred Scripture presents to us must be correctly interpreted. They show the complete frustration and emptiness of life without God. Rather than a place, hell indicates the state of those who freely and definitively separate themselves from God, the source of all life and joy. This is how the *Catechism of the Catholic Church* summarizes the truths of faith on this subject: "To die in mortal sin without repenting and accepting God's merciful love means remaining separated from him for ever by our own free choice. This state of definitive self-exclusion from communion with God and the blessed is called 'hell'" (n. 1033).

Chapter 13

Neither Here Nor There

A flame willing to light the torches of others will shine far brighter than those that choose to self-ignite.
Team Spirit

It was a cold winters evening a few years ago when I picked up Margareta for a three-hour drive in the rain. We were going to see a patient who was expected to soon make transition into the spirit world. This isn't normally something I do, due to the belief that I do not need to be physically there. But the family had called me and asked that we sit with them and do a meditation with Karen. She was only young and was passing from a brain tumour resulting from melanoma.

My guides encouraged me to go to the extent that they cancelled my other work for the evening. There was not only healing to be done but teaching as well. I agreed to attend to Karen, as my evening was now free. I explained to the family that a private room would be required and miraculously Karen was soon moved to her own room, without the hospital even knowing the intention. I'm sure this was divine intervention.

As Margareta and I arrived at the front doors of Palliative Care, Margareta hesitated to walk into the hospital. I asked her what was going on and she said she didn't want to go in. This totally surprised me as she was a gifted healer and was talking the whole three hours on the way of the wonderful energy she would give Karen in her transition. Her face showed emotions I had never seen before. We both realised in that moment she had not healed herself of the pain she'd been through nursing both her mother and father in their final stages on this side of life.

The spirit world knew all along that Margareta could never let me do this alone and like a dog on a chain she dragged her heels through the corridors until we got to Karen's room. Once we arrived, the responsibility of being a medium and a light for the spirit world became a realisation. The family looked to us for guidance and together we did a meditation by holding hands around Karen's bed and including her hands in the circle, too. It was a wonderful spiritual experience I will never forget and Karen's deceased loved ones were present as well.

As I looked across the room and saw Margareta glowing with light, it was the first time I had seen such tremendous love emanating from any human being. It's emotional for me to even write about it now. Margareta had never known Karen and neither did I. Margareta held onto Karen's feet, sending love and light through her body and telling her that everything was going to be fine. Margareta had forgotten about her own unfinished healing and Karen was teaching us all that nothing can ever separate us, even if we don't know one another in the physical world. All our spirits are united as one and that special feeling we all had that night was irreplaceable.

After a little while sitting with the family, I realised that Karen was starting to communicate with me. She had been in a coma state for a few days and I could hear her voice clearly speaking. I had never communicated with anyone before who had not completely passed over, so this was something new to me. I had no idea what to do, as I didn't want the family to think she had already gone over when she had clearly not.

I started to converse with the family by reciting conversations and events that had occurred that day in the room. The family was surprised at the information and so was I – as I began to tell them that Karen was the source of this knowledge. They accepted it and when I asked Karen where she was, she said she was in a beautiful field with flowers under her bare feet and ready to go soon. She had accepted her transition well and to my surprise she then said exactly the same words to the family as she had said just before she had slipped into a coma some days before. She had her own little way of telling them she loved them and in this instance she wanted to have the last word, too.

Karen was still physically alive that evening when Margareta and I left the hospital. We didn't speak that much on the long, late-night drive home as Karen had taught us both a lot and we were still processing our thoughts. The human side of us knew the time was definitely close and how brave she was to share this experience with us at a deeper soul level. I knew our work was done and the spirit world would take care of Karen, as obviously the whole evening was pre-guided for healing and teaching purposes.

A couple of days later my spirit guides informed me that Karen had made transition to the spirit world. Karen had started a new vibrant life with her loved ones on the other side. The family officially notified me of the news and I was relieved for Karen that she was active again and enjoying her new body, too. Her family attended the next platform and together we all remembered such a brave soul who was here to teach many to live life to the full – and that she did.

I believe that in the first year of passing over into the spirit world, many of your loved ones draw close to the earth plane and then move back into their own vibration more frequently than those who have been over for a few years. The reason for this is that they need to adjust to a new, non-material life and their minds, or consciousness, do not change that much when they pass over. If at the time of their passing they were interested in certain family activities, they will continue to observe them from their new world on a regular basis. There's nothing wrong with this – if your life was their life they'll continue to be a part of that in their own little way.

I don't believe that loved ones are floating around neither here nor there between the two worlds. There's a fine line between the two, as Karen has taught us. Karen was more on the spirit side than the physical side and so I was communicating with her spirit, who was starting to prepare for complete transition into that world. Once our loved ones pass over into the spirit world, there are continued transitional stages of healing as they build their own lives while at the same time continuing to be a part of ours.

The concept of being in limbo doesn't exist as part of my understanding of spirits. I know that when a newborn child comes into this world, he or she will often giggle and stare at the ceiling as they are still communicating with loved ones in the spirit world where their souls just came from. Are these babies in a limbo state? Of course not. They're simply adjusting to a new life on the physical plane with the assistance of grandparents and family members who looked after them in the spirit world before they were born into this world.

The same applies to my life in this world. My physical body communicates with the audience and I simply focus my attention on the living as well as their deceased loved ones in the spirit world. I simultaneously work with the varying vibrations of the two worlds together throughout the evening. I am neither here nor there and no longer limited by time and space as the spirit has no concept of this. So while your loved ones are living in the spirit world they can focus their attention on you as well, just like the medium does in a platform demonstration.

I was on my way to Germany again, this time to see Aunt Kate. The purpose of the journey was to visit her and to undertake some mediumship again in England. As I boarded the train from Cologne to Aachen, the flashbacks began. I remembered the first time Aunt Kate and Grandma picked me up from the station. Back then, the three of us laughed all the way to Aachen on the train and were excited that we would be spending Christmas together that year, plus a whole two months of quality time.

Looking back, I realised they were both in their early eighties and still as vibrant as ever and the strongest women I had ever known. Two sisters, only a year apart, and they reminded me so much of how Therese and I could be if we both survive to that age. They corrected my German language and sent me to the shops with complicated requests. But they believed in me, anything was possible, and we loved one another on a level that most people never experience in a whole lifetime with grandparents and aunty figures.

Then, my flashbacks focused on the last time I had been in Germany and at that train station. Grandma had passed away and I had arrived to help Dad sort out her remains and personal belongings. That same feeling came over me as I began to think of Aunt Kate and the week that was ahead of me in the mountains on my own. Aunt Kate had recently had a stroke and was now in an old people's home in the small mountain town of Zweifall.

Once I arrived at the hotel in Zweifall, I was excited to go and see Aunt Kate. She didn't speak on the phone when I called from Australia as she found it difficult. I would often just sing to her on the phone for long periods of time so she didn't need to respond. I sang the tunes that she taught me over the years and every now and then I would hear a small giggle on the phone, either when she had a memory, if I was out of tune or if the German word was said incorrectly. It didn't matter and we both knew that our spirits were united through harmony.

I could see the loneliness in so many faces as I walked through the doors of the old people's home. As a medium, I couldn't help but think how wonderful these people's transition into the spirit world would be. The party when they pass over would be fantastic as most of their friends are not on this side of life and their spirit body will be a replica of their own physical body at the prime of their life. How great must that be? No loneliness, no aches and pains and a new vibrant body to go with it.

When I found my way to Aunt Kate's room, I barely recognised her. There was nothing left of her in physical form and when she saw me she gave a smile and a tear before she moved into an unconscious state of sleep. She had not forgotten me and my idea to arrive unexpectedly was well worth the short surprised look on her face. As I sat with her for hours on the first day, there was hardly any response at all. Most of the time she was in a deep unconscious state with an occasional movement here and there.

On the morning of the second day, I became inspired. All inspiration comes from either our own spirits or someone else's. The source was irrelevant to me at that stage. I took a journey to the city of Aachen, where Grandma and Aunt Kate both lived for many years and where together we had many fond memories. I went to a department store and bought a small stereo player and all the German music I could find that I knew she would love. That afternoon, I carried it all into the old people's home and began my own party in Aunt Kate's room.

Before too long, she began to move her toes and that little giggle I would hear on the phone came back to life. I thought when I walked in the first day that she had already passed over, as she had no physical life in her at all. I wasn't there to speak to her physically, I was there to communicate with her spirit and her spirit loved the music. I was there to have my own farewell with her before her spirit made its way over to a new life. This was our little party and I could see that she was enjoying every moment of it and so was I.

That afternoon as I walked down the corridor, the old people nodded their heads with excitement, wondering who this noisy Australian kangaroo was, hopping and dancing around in Aunt Kate's room. I didn't care one bit as every part of me knew this would be the last time I would see Aunt Kate on this side of life. The next day her eyes were open as I walked into the room and she smiled in a way I will never forget. She didn't need to speak to me and her spirit was shining through her eyes and connecting with mine. Nothing could ever separate us, not even a 95-year-old body that was no longer functioning.

I had never met Aunt Kate's nephew Udo and I began to visualise how great it would be for all of us to be together on my last day there. To my surprise, within a day of thinking that, Udo arrived at the home at exactly the same time I was leaving for the day. We introduced ourselves and he said he would come back the next day, which was my last day in Germany.

When Udo and his wife arrived, we all held hands around Aunt Kate and laughed about the good old times with her and Grandma. Until the previous day I had never met Udo, just like I had never met Karen, but our souls connected at a time of need for all involved. I was not alone saying goodbye to Aunt Kate halfway across the world. I was together with other people who also loved her in their own way. It is this connection that's the true spirit of humanity, the realisation that we're all one, without the need to physically say it through words and complex cemented relationships.

Just before I left Aunt Kate, I gave a personal message of love from each and every family member in Australia. I mentioned their name, what they were currently doing and that they loved and cared for her deeply. She was not alone and everyone was thinking of her in his or her own little way. She smiled and her eyes knew the truth in these messages and together we said our final goodbyes with peace.

Exactly two months to the day after leaving Germany, I was inspired to do some spirit drawings. Dianne, my good friend and fellow medium, was more than willing to always go along with my experimentation with the spirit world. I wonder how she has put up with my enthusiasm over the years! I had some charcoal, paper and a little apron and I was ready to see if we could produce something different. One particular day, I was inspired and motivated so much I told my boss before I left work that something special was going to happen that evening.

I hadn't spoken to Dianne for at least two weeks and when I arrived we sat down quietly in a room together. As I began to move into an altered trance state, blindfolded and not knowing what to expect, within seconds my hand automatically produced the most wonderful drawing of a dog. The two of us were in disbelief as it was perfect and there was no way I could have drawn it myself, let alone blindfolded and in the dark! We both began to laugh as neither of us recognised the dog.

Within moments, I heard very clearly on the right side of me, "*It's Moppee.*" I was now completely in shock, especially after the voice then said, "*It's Kate.*" My heart dropped in disbelief at what I was hearing. The last words I said to Aunt Kate were, "*I love you Moppee,*" which was her nickname in German. I told Dianne what I was hearing and I said, "*I think Aunt Kate has passed over.*" In moments I became aware of an old man standing next to me as well. He said his name was William and he wanted to tell Dianne he had arrived okay in the spirit world.

This was all a bit much for us. I hadn't spoken to Dianne for two weeks, so I wasn't up to date with her news. She had apparently been upset about an old man who had passed away that week, before she had a chance to say goodbye. Dianne volunteers her services at an old people's home and she goes there with her dogs to provide comfort to the residents. I know she's been sent there for a higher purpose, a beacon of light before they all make their transition into the spirit world.

She confirmed that the man had indeed passed away a few days earlier. She had yelled out loudly in the car to him while driving home that day, *"You could have waited until I got there to say goodbye!"* Well, he came back and said his goodbyes all right – flirting with my 95-year-old Aunt Kate and leaving us both in a state of shock we will never forget. I have since framed the dog drawing and believe it was one of the greatest gifts the spirit world has ever given to me. Shortly after, I received the news from Germany that Aunt Kate did indeed pass away unexpectedly, approximately half an hour before her appearance here.

As I'm completing this chapter, I know it's not a coincidence that I'm sharing this story today, at a time when two of my close friends are experiencing similar circumstances. Marie, my work colleague, has an overseas aunt in much the same state as Aunt Kate and she's very close to her as well. I advised her just the other day to call her and send a recorded audio message so she can hear her voice. She will hear this regardless of the state she's in. Hearing is the last physical sense to go before we pass over into the spirit world.

Elke, one of my greatest helpers and a gifted healer and dear friend on this side of life, is experiencing the same situation with her mother. Her mother is also German, she has a brother by the name of Udo who has passed into the spirit world and I know her mother will make transition when the timing is ready for her soul. Elke also helps old people and lately she's been taking kittens in to see the residents, which has brought them all to life again. The youth of the kittens is a reminder to them of how vibrant our spirits are when we're carefree about life. Cats have nine lives and so do we, more lives that we can ever imagine since life is eternal and so is the gift of love. This is why we call those closest to our heart our "loved ones".

Just when I thought this chapter was finished, my spirit guides asked me to call Elke that evening and tell her that this chapter was a gift from the spirit world. I had not shared the book with anyone until then. I always wondered why little of Elke had been mentioned up until now, even though she had played an important role in assisting with my mediumship events and healing. I did as spirit asked and shared the chapter with Elke and she absolutely loved it.

The following morning at 1.30am, Elke's mum passed into the spirit world. Elke had received a gift just like my spirit drawing – a reminder of how much of our lives are pre-ordained – and how the spirit world takes care of everything in advance. I could now see the power in the chapter and the teaching the spirit world was trying to convey to the readers and their indirect preparation for both Elke and I.

Over the next few days, both Elke and I relived the events of this chapter. A couple of days later, I found myself driving three hours again to the exact same location where Karen passed away to attend

Elke's mum Ilse's funeral. What were the chances? Apart from these two events, I had never been in that location in my life. On the long drive to the funeral, two of my helpers, Marisia and Anastasia, began to bring up their own unfinished healing with their mothers and how they had not addressed their deaths since their passing. It was almost identical to Margareta not wanting to come through the hospital doors when attending to Karen. The similarities were beginning to unfold and upon arriving at the cemetery for Ilse's funeral, a German priest with the strongest accent began to speak. I had flashbacks again to Germany and when the name Udo was mentioned (Elke's brother) it became more real.

Elke had lost two brothers, Udo and Jurgen. Udo passed by drowning, the same way as my brother, and he shares the name of the cousin I met on my last day with Aunt Kate. Jurgen passed in a mining accident and shares a second name with my father. As I stood at the funeral near Ilse's grave, right next to her were the graves of two brothers, totally unrelated to Ilse, who passed very young and a few years apart. It was confirmation to me that Ilse was now happy with her two boys in the spirit world.

Elke is so dedicated to spirit that within three days of her mother's passing, she still attended my public platform demonstration and helped with everything as she normally does. She put aside her own grief and wanted to be in the place where she felt closest to her mum's spirit. Even though her mother didn't come through the platform, there were powerful messages in all the readings for the audience that shared more gifts and teaching from the spirit world.

A lady at the back of the room had lost her mother in similar circumstances and she came from the same place as where the funeral was held, some three hours away. There were very specific details in all the readings that were exactly the same as Ilse's life and passing. This also included the forgiveness she needed to give to find peace and the humorous flashing of personal body parts that we will not mention in detail here! Lots of humour and healing came through that evening and at the end of the platform my guides reminded me that it would be Mother's Day that weekend. This showed me the greater purpose in all of this teaching in this chapter.

Through my events, Elke's events and the events of the mothers in spirit who came through platform that week, my spirit guides were re-emphasising the importance of surrender. Just as a mother gives birth to a child, they trust that the child will come into this world in their own time. The same applies when the spirit decides to enter the spirit world again. This timing is pre-ordained and for most of the people passing over it's only known to their human-self just moments before making the transition.

No matter how hard you attempt to be there for the birthing of a child into this world or the birthing of your loved ones into the spirit world, it is predetermined who will be physically present. It doesn't matter if you're physically there or not as the spirit is never limited but can be everywhere at once. The spirit world, through Aunt Kate's passing overseas, had more than proven this. You may not be aware of this consciously but on a deeper soul level you have already welcomed or said goodbye to one another in the knowing that one day you will reunite in the world of spirit again.

Chapter 14

Chook

"Light" footprints leave the greatest impressions.
Team Spirit

It was the early hours of the morning, in Newcastle, when I was woken by a clear vision. I saw my twin sister, Therese, with her cat Gargamelle sitting on her stomach. The cat was dressed in a baby bonnet and bib as well as having a dummy in its mouth. Just when I thought I was going completely mad, the bed I was lying on completely disappeared in my vision and out of the room. Looking back, I should have had some idea what it all meant but at the time I just laughed off the strangeness of it all.

Some time later, I had an out-of-body experience and found myself in an old house that I grew up in as a child. I was in the bathroom of the house and could clearly see a baby's face that had not yet formed. The baby was lying in an old bath and standing behind was my grandmother in spirit, smiling. I knew in an instant there was a child coming into the family and the bond we would have together would be at a very deep level.

It was soon confirmed that Therese was indeed pregnant and now the vision in the room made sense. Therese had no children and since she had often said that Gargamelle was her baby, spirit was attempting to tell me something. My bed disappearing meant that the room I stayed in on weekends on Therese's property was to be converted into a baby room to accommodate the new soul entering our lives.

I often see spirits of babies in the early months of pregnancies, most of the time before the mother is even aware they're around. I'm very careful not to share this information and just wait for it to be confirmed in the physical world. Sometimes things can change in those early months, so I'm well aware of the sensitivities of the topic.

Most of the time when I do see those little souls, their faces are not completely formed to me and sometimes I can't tell their sex. They all seem to look the same and there are even times when they show themselves as a small child, up to seven years of age. I find it fascinating that they can project themselves to me so far into the future and as the years go by I actually do see them grow up in exactly the same vision as I had seen before their birth. This occurred with my work colleague Kathleen's daughter, who I discussed earlier in the book.

From my understanding of the spirit world, I know that little of the soul does connect with the womb in the early stages of pregnancy. The soul of the child moves back and forth between the womb and the spirit world and it's not until the birth of the child into this world that the soul completely attaches itself to its own auric field. The reason for this is that its physical body needs to be completely away from the physical body and aura of the mother for this full individual connection to occur.

This doesn't mean that babies have no souls. That's not true. It just means that up until birth they live between both the spirit world and the physical world. Mothers can feel more emotional at the times when there's a lot of movement between the two worlds as the baby is re-entering from a world of love. Throughout this period of movement, the soul of the baby is in constant contact with deceased relatives on the other side.

This is why so many babies and toddlers recognise deceased loved ones through photos or seeing spirits they have never met on this side of life. The babies have just come from their world and have spent plenty of time with them as well. When someone passes over while there's a pregnancy on this side of life, no relatives are missing out at all. Everyone is involved, on both sides of life, as throughout this period the baby is not limited by time and space. It's not much different to when people are passing over into the spirit world. This is a natural part of transition both in and out of the spirit world.

Now if a baby doesn't physically survive full term or is stillborn, it will go through the normal process of physical death like any other child. The soul may decide to return again in an attempt at another pregnancy, or it may decide to grow up slowly with the deceased relatives on the other side. Either way, the soul has the chance to grow up again in this world or in the spirit world.

This may surprise you but there are plenty of people passing over into the spirit world after many years on this side of life to find that they have a child in the spirit world who has now grown up. They may not have been aware of the pregnancy in the first place, they may have had an abortion, or perhaps the child was given away at birth and has since passed away. There's no judgement in the spirit world – not even about abortions – and it's up to you if you wish to pursue your relationship with them further once you pass over. There are even nurseries in the spirit world that allow young mothers who did not have the chance to have children here to raise these children as their own. No child is ever lost as all children are nurtured with care.

A well known international medium lost a small baby at a very young age some years ago and did not get over the death of the child. One evening, the spirit world took her to the other side to meet the boy. She also discovered that she had miscarried twins, a boy and a girl, many years before and they had grown up in the spirit world. She didn't recognise the twins and had no idea of their existence. When she returned to the earth plane, she felt an immense amount of guilt as she still favoured her little boy with whom she shared a physical life. The spirit world empathised with this and they understand it is difficult for someone to comprehend these souls while living a life on the earth plane.

Given that there needs to be carers and even guides for these baby souls on their new journey on earth, it's not uncommon for an adult, such as a parent or grandparent, to pass over around the time of the physical birth of a child. I believe this is all part of the divine contract among souls to enter and exit this life with a greater purpose to guide and teach one another on their soul evolution. I see a lot of this in my readings and it's wonderful knowing that these souls have spent many lifetimes together sharing one another's journeys.

Therese was now seven months pregnant and her partner Shane was serving overseas in Iraq. Whenever I could, I would go to the property on weekends to give Therese a hand with any of the jobs that needed doing around the place. Therese never overstrained herself and she enjoyed the months of pregnancy. Shane would receive news on the progress of the baby over the phone and I have no doubt that the distance would have bonded them together on another level.

I had organised a short holiday with my sisters in a warmer state where we would all enjoy the sun. Once we arrived, Therese and I decided to celebrate our birthday a day early with a dinner across the road from the resort. Before we left, I told Therese that I had a terrible feeling inside me and I decided not to drink that night. I rarely drink alcohol anyway, but it was my birthday, I wasn't pregnant and no driving was necessary as we were only going down the road. Normally a drink on this occasion is something I would consider, however I decided not to.

Once she had finished dinner, Therese said she wanted to go home a little earlier than planned. After dropping her off, the rest of us went across the road to listen to some music and I left early. I climbed into bed with Therese and shortly afterwards she woke up bleeding. Therese was seven months pregnant and I had no idea what to do.

Before leaving for the holiday, I had booked a rental car for the week. The resort was across the road from the beach, so there was no real use for it. However, that evening the car was appreciated as we rushed Therese to the hospital. It was lucky I was with Therese in the bed that night and lucky that we had the car as well. Her placenta had ruptured and the baby may have been coming sooner than expected.

The baby's lungs had not yet formed and there was concern that an early birth could place enormous risk on its life. I trusted in Team Spirit to assist Therese where they could and that everything would work out according to plan. After a few days in hospital, the bleeding stopped and Therese was released to enjoy a couple of days of fresh air at the resort. I knew in my heart that she was going to be okay and for the next two months we were all on standby in case of another bleed.

It was not a coincidence that I had organised to be with Therese that week. I would normally have been some hours away in Sydney and Therese would have been alone at the property with Shane away. A couple of months later, I was prompted again to go home to Newcastle a day earlier than usual. Within hours of arrival, Therese had another bleed. With Shane home, the three of us headed to the hospital ready for the grand entry of a child I had met many months earlier.

I had my secret bag with the "It's a Boy" stocking ready to pin up. I had total confidence it was a boy, even with no formal scans to confirm it. I kept my knowingness to myself to allow those involved to be surprised. I didn't plan to be there at his birth and I fell asleep in the chair amongst all the chaos and ended up staying in the room for the long birth. Bryce was born a healthy boy at 9.50pm on Christmas Eve on a blue moon. I would know him as "Chook" and he would change my life forever.

Once Bryce arrived, the placenta ruptured and Therese was sent for emergency surgery. The surgeon's words were that the bleeding was like torrential rain and they thought she would not survive. Shane followed Therese to surgery and I was left with Chook for around an hour. I was calm and every part of me knew Therese was going to be okay and this baby, who I had met before, was here as a part of that journey, too. This special time Chook and I had together alone when he arrived that evening, felt the same as when we first met in my out-of-body experience. He didn't speak to me but our souls connected on another level. It was now midnight Christmas Eve and Chook was the best present to come into my life.

Therese and Bryce are now doing well. Chook is almost three years old and through his experience he has taught me so much. He has shown me that it was not his time to go and that he was arriving for an experience here on earth. Intervention had occurred on a number of occasions for this very reason. Now whenever I experience people losing hope through the medical problems of a child, or even through the physical loss of a child, I always remind myself of the power of Chook's arrival.

I believe that sometimes souls are sent here for a very short period of time to bring about lessons, hope and even to open the hearts and minds of people around them. Some of these are more advanced souls who are sent to evolve humanity on many different levels. If they do not eventually grow up as children or are not even born on this side of life, I know they will grow up slowly in the spirit world and be nurtured by deceased relatives. A miscarried or stillborn child is never lost.

Nothing can ever take a baby away from its mother or family. He or she will always be around, giggling, laughing, playing and having fun. When babies move over to the spirit world, there is little transition for their souls as they have just come from that peaceful place. This is why children are so spirited and innocent – they have not yet been corrupted by the human ego beliefs on this side of life. A soul of a child reminds us who we truly are, with the power of the human spirit shining in its greatest essence of life.

Chapter 15

Children and Animal Spirits

A heart of gold at the end of the rainbow is worth much more than a pot of gold.
Team Spirit

One day, in the early hours of the morning, an Aboriginal lady in spirit woke me up with a distinctive message for her granddaughter. She was accompanied by a tall man with snow-white hair and together they told me that their granddaughter must take natural remedies for the little child who was waiting in the spirit world to be born. Their love for this soul to come into the world was immense and I felt an overwhelming sense of responsibility to deliver the message. The problem was I had no idea who the message was for and the couple seemed to have left without giving me this critical piece of information.

Late that morning, I documented my experience with the couple during the night and folded it away in the trust that the rest of the information would come forward naturally in time. I assumed the pair would be back as their energy was extremely strong and the Aboriginal lady was definitely a persistent character. If the message was meant to be delivered, the opportunity would come forward as it did in all my work with the spirit world.

It was my day off from mediumship and I was ready to enjoy a day out with some girlfriends. It was my good friend Maryanne's hens' day – we were celebrating her marriage to come in the next few weeks. The weather was perfect, the sun was shining and it was a beautiful summer's day near the water in Sydney. The atmosphere was perfect for relaxation and I really did look forward to having some quality time with the living, too.

My wish was short-lived. A lady arrived at the lunch and sat on the other side of the room. I was immediately aware of the spirits of the Aboriginal lady and the tall man as they wanted me to speak to the woman right away. Can you imagine it? I didn't know the lady or any of the people around her and they wanted me to introduce myself through them. I also found it difficult to picture the spirits being her grandparents, since the Aboriginal lady was dark in complexion and the man was tall and very fair. The lady I was to introduce myself to didn't look like she had Aboriginal ancestry at all so I really did need to trust the spirits, as on every other occasion.

I walked over and sat at the table near the woman. I quickly introduced myself and she told me her name was Jessica. Like tearing a bandaid off a wound, I quickly blurted out the description of her grandparents and the message they had from the spirit world. If I had the wrong person I could just run back to my table. She would just think I'd had too much wine and that the heat had taken it all to my head. To my surprise, she smiled at me and began to cry. She knew very well who the two spirits were and laughed at the prospect of their visit. She hadn't told anyone that she had already bought some natural remedies to start the following week in the hope of falling pregnant. She was so excited that she immediately called her mother with the news.

That day I enjoyed myself with the girls in the summer sun and Jessica and I seemed to have bonded on another level. She is a lovely girl with a beautiful heart and I was excited at her suggestion that she send me her grandparents' photo the following week. When I opened the email, I laughed and said, *"Yep, that's them – they're the two amigos that kept me up all night!"* Their distinctive facial features were evident and not many Aboriginal women marry tall, fair men with snow-white hair. As for not providing me with the recipient of the message, there was no need for them to do that. Their love for their granddaughter was so strong they had broken through many barriers, including my day off from mediumship, to take me directly to her.

Soon after, Jessica had a beautiful baby girl and the assistance of her grandparents and the persistence of that little soul is enough to make you realise the power of the human spirit. These souls from another world come to introduce themselves well before the mother is even aware of their arrival. This contractual agreement that exists is known by so many people in the spirit world and the love these little children have growing up throughout their lives here on earth should never be forgotten. The deceased loved ones are the caretakers throughout their lives in the spirit world and I believe there are assigned caretakers on this side of life for children as well.

Just as there are guides, angels and caretakers for children in the spirit world, I strongly believe these people also exist on this side of life. They are souls who stand strong in the belief that children should be protected and they have no conditional attachment to the child. I believe that my sister Tanya and our mutual friends April and Michele are assigned caretakers for these little souls. I know that when they eventually pass over into the spirit world they will not only guide their own children and grandchildren on this side of life but also many children spirits on the other side who require this unique love.

I remember someone saying to me one evening that it's a shame that I do not yet have children of my own, as I may never experience unconditional love. To my surprise, my guides quickly responded that the statement was not correct. They said that some of the love for children is conditional and the term unconditional is used too loosely on the earth plane. They quickly advised me that true unconditional love is when you are willing to swap your child with the parent of another child across the road and love them the same. If you can't do this, then the love for your child is conditional to the fact that the child shares your genetics and you have ensured that your own personal existence in physical form continues on throughout this side of life.

Children, on the other hand, are the ones who demonstrate unconditional love more often than parents. Children affect many people around them, including strangers who walk on the street. A smile, a wave or a silly gesture will move any soul around them, no matter how difficult life may be. Children will hug and kiss people they have never met and do not care about conditions or attachments such as race, religion or sexuality. It is this innocence, the pureness and naivety of the human spirit that makes the physical loss of a child so unbearable for most.

I have had many children come through my platform and I have thoroughly enjoyed each of the readings. Sometimes they can be the most difficult to communicate with, especially if they are of toddler age. Providing evidence and names doesn't seem to be high on the agenda of a small child, so sometimes I ask for the assistance of an adult spirit to provide this information. The children are, however, quick to tell on someone who has done something wrong and say things that are totally hilarious for the person I'm reading for. Their evidence can be brilliant in many other ways, too, as they can provide such detail of an event, including exactly what the people were wearing and what they were doing at the time. They're still observing closely in the spirit world and don't seem to have any feelings of separation between here or there. They didn't spend too much time on this side of life, so their minds are not corrupted by the limitations of thought that are conditions of the earth plane.

One evening, a little girl around the age of seven came onto the platform and said she was an angel. I listened to her and she provided further evidence, telling me about her passing. Her mother raised her hand and confirmed that the little girl's name was Angelica – that indeed confirmed her little angel story. She had passed through collapsing on the floor while playing and she didn't seem to be too concerned about all that. Her vibrant personality had everyone sitting in silence as she provided observations and evidence from her world. She also gave permission to donate a specific doll of hers for the spirit children to play with while doing platform.

Some time later, Lisa brought in the doll to donate to our platform. I hadn't spoken to her at all and when she arrived at the event she sat towards the back of the room. At the end of the evening, my guides asked that I remind the audience of the importance of children in our lives and the song *Over the Rainbow* was chosen for meditation. Lisa didn't notice that when she first sat down, right above her head was a drawing a living child had done of a rainbow. We were all surprised when we noticed it later on. The following day was the anniversary of Angelica's passing and although she hadn't spoken to anyone, Lisa had chosen the words in the song *Over the Rainbow* as part of Angelica's memorial.

Like many of the spirit children that come through platform, Angelica reminds us all that life shouldn't be a chore or an existence on a day-to-day basis. Life is an adventure that has no ending. It is this no-ending, no concept of time and space that allows children to capture true spiritual experiences whilst here on earth. The spirit world is one of mental thought, and imagination is the basis of creativity of that experience. Children are natural creators of their own reality and by observing their behaviour you will have a clearer idea of how your deceased loved ones live in the spirit world.

The loss of a child at a young age on earth does not only create grief about the fact that their life span was short and certain milestones were not achieved – it is much more than that. It is the loss of the reminder of who we truly are and what life is all about. Children create their own reality and happiness through thoughts, feelings and imagination that most adults have shut down throughout their lives.

When a child moves from this world to the spirit world, very little will change in their reality. Their transition will be easier than that of adults, as their imagination and creativity will just continue to blossom in a world that will accept all mental thoughts as real. Children will not be told to close down their imaginations and that such beautiful things do not exist, for they will exist for all children and adults if it be their request.

When thinking of children in the spirit world, think of them in an atmosphere that's more suited to their own mental reality. If you're an adult who has simply lost your way here on earth, take the time to observe the children and reflect on your own inner child. He or she will soon take you on a journey through the loss of time and space that will allow your spirit to be reignited and for you to live the life you truly deserve.

Apart from Angelica, there have been many powerful child spirits who have been sent to teach the audiences about forgiveness and unconditional love. A little seven-year-old girl who drowned in her backyard came through the platform to tell her mum to stop blaming herself. Her mum had faced so much grief and pain that it was time to let it go so she could live a normal life again. The little girl provided some wonderful evidence of names and observations from her world and wanted people to know that the drowning was just a few pages in the last chapter of her life. She had a wonderful life before that and understood that the experience was part of a greater plan. Some of these child spirits are so wise that I know they're more evolved souls that were sent here to teach.

I have had many instances of children passing in car accidents, illnesses and other tragic events that leave family members and friends with immense amounts of guilt. The children don't like to see this and after asking their loved ones to let it all go, they quickly go on to speak about their new lives in the spirit world. They have moved past the healing stages of physical death and it's important for them to see that those who are left behind here will also go through the healing process. They know more than anything that everyone will meet up again soon and with no concept of time and space, a lifetime here is just a drop in the ocean over there.

I have seen the power of parents coming together after the loss of a child and the immense amount of healing that can be obtained by connecting with one another on this side of life. A young lady in spirit by the name of Carla came through one of my audiences some years ago and she also brought through another young girl who had passed into spirit. Both connected with their mothers and that provided everyone involved with an immense amount of healing.

After a long period of time and now demonstrating in another location, I vaguely recognised a lady sitting in the audience who seemed to be at all the readings with children. Given that I have seen tens of thousands of people, I barely remember anyone, let alone the spirits as well. Reading after reading, there she was and it wasn't until some time later that she told me she was bringing along other mothers who had also lost their children. Of course we never discussed details, as it would ruin any evidence the spirits would bring forward in the future. I try to remain as impartial as I can. The woman was Sonya, Carla's mother and she's now a proud supporter of the work of the spirit world. Sonya sees dragonflies when her daughter is around and that wonderful sign reminds her of the beauty of Carla and her new life.

I believe strongly that Sonya now works for the spirit world in her own way. One day I was reading for a lady by the name of Wendy, who had lost a great niece in a car accident. The little girl's name in spirit was Sarah and she arrived in a fairy outfit, ready to communicate. Wendy's deceased relatives, who were of Aboriginal descent, clearly acknowledged that Sarah was fine in the spirit world and the evidence of this was great throughout her lovely reading.

At the end of the reading, the spirit world interrupted and asked that Wendy contact Sonya, who would be of assistance. Wendy had never met Sonya and they were from different areas so I tracked down the phone number and handed it over. That evening, after completing a day of readings, I was prompted by the spirit world to hire out a movie to watch. It was called *Fireflies in the Garden*. I soon found out why I had been led to watch that particular movie. It was about a young boy who ran out onto the road and caused the death of his aunt – resulting in much pain for the family.

The similarities between the reading earlier in the day with Sarah and the movie were immense. There was a strong quote in the movie: *"Sometimes a family must be torn apart before it can come together."* It emphasised that there are many factors that need to be aligned to bring about an event, not just one factor or one person. It's all about a greater plan to bring about an outcome and not just one person can be responsible for the outcome. Life is a play that has many actors. Some actors will play the lead and others the supporting roles.

The following week, Wendy decided to bring Sarah's mum, Anne, to a platform event for healing. There were around 150 chairs in the room that night – all full with unreserved seating. Anne chose a particular chair to sit in and upside-down on the chair was an angel card. Sometimes I place these cards that I buy in random packets on the chairs so everyone walks away with a personal message each evening. The angel card said, *"Sonya: Your deceased relatives are saying hello from the spirit world."* Sonya was a name of an angel that was clearly printed on the card as well.

After the event, Anne was introduced to Sonya and it was no doubt through divine intervention from the spirit world that these two people were brought together. Anne had been driving the car at the time of the accident and the "Sonya" card had validated that the spirit world were not punishing her for the physical death of Sarah. Rather, they had brought someone forward who had been through pain themselves through the loss of a child in a car accident. Sonya could assist Anne with the grieving process. Sarah was doing fine and nothing could ever separate the love the family had both for their little fairy and for each other.

It was later on that Anne shared another amazing twist to this whole story. A man who was at the scene of the accident went home and told his wife about the incident and he thought at the time that no-one was injured. His wife, a few weeks after the accident, handed Wendy a flyer with angels at the top of it. The flyer was information about my platform event and so Wendy came along with some Aboriginal friends. Those friends were read that night and it was the beginning of bridging their two worlds together as one.

Apart from fairies and dragonflies arriving from the spirit world, plenty of animals make their way over to greet their loved ones in readings. Most of these encounters I find quite fascinating as animals communicate quite differently in spirit than they do here. I'm a great animal lover, having grown up with horses, cats and dogs all my life. We tend to communicate more with feelings and emotions with animals than other living things.

I believe that in the spirit world, animals play a very different role in companionship than here on the earth plane. From my understanding, their level of intelligence receives much more respect than on earth. They communicate their thoughts directly in a unique way. When you do talk to the animals they will respond but not in a bark or language that you won't understand. They will speak to you in a way that you completely understand. It's very difficult for me to explain and I have encountered it many times.

On platform, I will identify a particular animal through description, name and other details. The animal may then blend its energy further with me and I will be able to give very specific details of what it liked, bad habits and other attributes that are an instant knowingness that's hard to explain in words. The animal doesn't tell me this. I just know when it gives me a type of permission to surrender this information. Some animals are not interested in this at all and just want to come and sit near their owners at platform events to be with them. And no, I don't see dogs fighting with cats in my audiences.

Most of the encounters I've had with animal spirits have been quite funny. My mum lives with a man who is part of the family and known to us as Graeme. After the passing of Buffy, my Mum and Graeme's dog, his spirit quickly made himself known within 24 hours of transition to the spirit world. His features were very distinguished and I had no idea what the white and grey, spiky fur ball flash was behind him. Upon investigation I soon realised that the fur ball was Tammy, who was a feral cat that Mum and Graeme had saved some years before. The spikes were the thistles she always had in her hair as a wandering cat in her earlier years. I suppose she enjoyed those days and still does in the spirit world.

I know that my spirit guides must laugh at my requests when an animal passes into the spirit world. I light a candle for them just like I do for humans and one day they clearly showed me with humour that they do listen to all my requests. My sister Tanya called one day, distressed that her dog of 15 years, Zoe, was very unwell and would soon be passing. My guides indicated that Zoe would make the transition soon, everything would be taken care of on their side and we should simply surrender.

My sister did surrender and Zoe passed away peacefully into the spirit world that afternoon. Around 2am the next morning, I was woken by sounds in the bathroom. As I walked into the bathroom, Zoe was sitting backwards to the door and seemed to be smiling as her head turned. She was very happy and one of my guides giggled when he realised I had gotten the message. Zoe's nickname was space cadet – we always said she looked like she'd just been captured by a UFO and dumped in the middle of nowhere. Well, she did look like a space cadet that morning – my bathroom was in Sydney and her house was in Newcastle! Her body was positioned in a weird, backward pose like she had just been dumped out of thin air.

One evening on platform, a spirit of a very big white horse was standing in the aisle of the audience. It loved its owner so much that she just wanted to let her know she was there. The name of the horse was also given to me and the owner quickly raised her hand and acknowledged her attendance. No other evidence was necessary as I provided details of a distinguishing mark on her body as well.

Ginger Meggs was my horse of 25 years and I loved her to bits. I grew up riding her all the time and she spent most of her retired blissful years on Therese's property. She was diagnosed with liver cancer and I clearly remember the morning she stopped me in my tracks literally as I drove back to the property to make one of the hardest decisions of my life. She told me that morning as I was leaving and driving back to Sydney that she'd had enough and was ready to leave behind her deteriorating physical body. Her wish was granted and the day was a beautiful experience for both Therese and I, as we lay on her stomach in the long grass as she was put to sleep.

Therese was at the front of my platform one evening when, unexpectedly, Ginger Meggs made herself known to her. Therese said it was the closest she ever felt to any spirit, including human beings. Ginger came and told her that she was fine and happy where she was. Ginger must have known that Therese always thought of her in the mornings when she attended to the other horses. I have since seen Ginger Meggs and she has come with great love and messages in many ways. We have a deep soul connection that can never be torn apart through physical loss.

I believe that animals and children are the greatest teachers in spirit to all humanity. They love unconditionally, do not judge, do not care how much money we have in our bank accounts or even what we wear. They don't gossip about small things in life that are irrelevant, they never leave this life arguing and leaving behind unfinished business and they're the first to come through readings and forgive the most unforgivable things.

They understand the true essence of the spirit and that life never ends. Their transition into the spirit world seems much more seamless to me as they understand to the core what life is all about. They don't care whether or not you're in physical form, for they know that the physical body is just a shell for a temporary experience. A temporary experience that can impress everlasting teaching and learning for the souls who have been left behind on the earth plane.

Chapter 16

Can Spirit Predict?

An empty tank is better filled through self-service rather than the reliance of pumping from others.
Team Spirit

Upon commencing a new chapter this evening, I am even surprised at the unpredictability of my spirit guides while writing this book. Last night, I was prompted by the spirit world to write the previous chapter with a sense of urgency. I have never written any of this book content on weeknights – I only dedicate my weekends to writing, since it can be very tiring. Listening to the spirit world last night as usual, I wrote the whole chapter in just a few hours.

In the early hours this morning, my spirit guides prompted me to check my email and advised that there was a little teaching twist. At the exact time I was writing the previous chapter, an email was sent to me in relation to Anne's court case. Apparently I had advised Wendy to tell Anne some months ago that a star would be given to her from Sarah and she needed to take this into the courtroom with her.

A lady by the name of Glenys gave Anne a specific angel star, which signifies children who have passed away. Yesterday was the actual court case – I had no idea at all, since the reading was months ago and the date had not yet been determined. Anne held the star very tightly in the courtroom yesterday and the judge decided to give no conviction for the accidental death of Sarah. Anne had enough to face for the rest of her life and she intended no harm to Sarah.

Sonya had provided support to Anne and her family and, in an ironic twist, Sonya had lost her own daughter in a car accident. I know this court case was also an important part of Sonya's own healing and my spirit guides sent her to Anne's family to teach the remarkable act of forgiveness. Was this meeting all pre-ordained by the spirit world for not only the healing of those involved but also the healing of so many people reading this book? Of course it was – and this story in itself provides confirmation to me once again that there is a direct correlation between the ability to predict with high levels of accuracy and the intention and purpose of healing.

It's very common for me to hear, "*You should know that, Louise, you're a psychic.*" But most of the time I have no idea, like the rest of you, who will win a football game, if someone will be attending a party or if the storms will clear tomorrow. A psychic is someone who tunes into the vibrations of the living people and the earth. It would take a lot of time and effort to even attempt to tune into such answers, of which I have no interest in at all. If it serves no purpose of healing, then I simply will not focus my attention on the result. Also, I have a life, too, and I like to live it day to day like everyone else and enjoy the little surprises that make life so special. Just like the surprise of the chapter last night, it has had me on a little high all day, knowing the power of my spirit team and the greater healing purpose of mediumship.

I believe a psychic does not require the assistance of the spirit world. They can attune into the vibrational frequency of the earth plane and provide information to the sitter on such matters as relationships, health and perhaps even a prediction here and there. They are very much like a general practitioner doctor who can work alone without the assistance of a team in the spirit world.

A medium, however, requires the assistance of guides from the spirit world. For me, these guides are known as Team Spirit. A medium can sit with someone and tune into their loved ones on the other side in the spirit world, as well as provide psychic information. For an individual reading, the medium is like a surgeon who has been trained as a doctor (psychic) and has the option to switch skills (to mediumship) depending on the requirements of the sitter. All surgeons (mediums) must have the qualifications to be a doctor first (psychic) but not all doctors (psychics) are trained as surgeons (mediums).

A platform medium who demonstrates to audiences and connects with the spirit world is another extension of this skill level. The surgeon (medium) has specialist skills that involve greater levels of focus and commitment to their work and to provide healing to the masses in need. This would be the equivalent of a brain surgeon performing an operation for hours with a team of helpers in the room (Team Spirit). A brain surgeon (platform medium) needs to be a surgeon (medium) first but also has the skills of a doctor (psychic).

A brain surgeon (platform medium) will always prefer to work on those in greater need of healing (for example, brain tumours) than to provide general doctor work to people (for example, prescriptions). It doesn't make general practitioner (psychic) work less meaningful – it just means their purpose and training by the spirit world is to provide mediumship to the masses. Since there are a lot less brain surgeons (platform mediums) than general doctors (psychics), you can now see why I choose to do minimal psychic work as this can be picked up by others who have a greater level of interest and focus in this area.

I do however believe that psychic predictions can also be very limiting. If the person receiving the information obtains it on the vibrations of the earth plane without the assistance of the spirit world, their ability to predict with high possibility may not occur all the time. The reason for this is that their viewpoint of certain events may be limited by the predictability of certain players in those events and the free will and choices of those involved.

Someone such as me, who is consistent in my decision-making processes in life, would perhaps make less radical changes in choices than someone who is up and down all the time in their decision-making process. In the event of a prediction made by a psychic, one person's radical changes in their choices can turn the outcome of the event completely around. The psychic may not necessarily be wrong; the prediction may have been based on the current choices they could see with certain players.

This is my understanding of how predictions work and I don't expect everyone else to agree. I'm just sharing with you my own experiences with the spirit world through what their teachings have provided to me. I am a very scientifically minded person as well and I have an interest in this topic. When I have asked these questions to my spirit guides over the years, they have set up experiments with me to draw me to these conclusions. If people understood these mechanics then perhaps they would be less harsh on psychics attempting to provide predictions.

One morning, I was woken by Team Spirit as they showed me in a vision the winner of the biggest horse race in Australia, which was to be run that day. I was pretty excited as I saw the horse go over the line and they advised me of an exact amount of money I should place on the horse to purchase a gift from them to me in the physical world. That day, I went to the races with all my friends and kept the winner to myself as it was given to me for a higher purpose.

Team Spirit was now betting in the physical world and I was excited at the prospect that the gift they were purchasing would be the new chairs for my platform events to accommodate the growing public demand. After the horse went over the line, I left my friends and on the way home I checked the ticket. We had only won a small amount of money and as I collected it, Team Spirit asked me to walk directly across the road. I couldn't see any shops selling chairs. They asked me to walk into a specific store.

The shop I walked into was a women's clothing store and they flashed in my vision their gift. There on the rack was a beautiful blue top with angel wings at the back. It was gorgeous and when I checked the price, it was exactly the same amount as we'd won in the horse race. I couldn't believe it and they soon advised me it was a gift from the spirit world to wear for my upcoming 100th audience event. They have asked for this shirt to be pictured on the front cover of this book as a reminder that gifts can come in so many different ways.

Now I knew my team could predict horse races from a much higher level, I asked them to show me if deceased loved ones could also predict large events with such accuracy. This would assist me in developing a theory on predictions and the myths that psychics should be able to win lotto and other chance events. Given that I only go to the horse races a couple of times a year, it was around 12 months later that I obtained some more powerful teaching on the topic of predictions.

I was at the horse races with some very good friends, when the spirit of a man known as Vince made himself known to me. His daughter, Jodie, was standing next to me and I let her know that her father was chatting to me about a specific horse known as Number 3 that would win the big event the following week. He told me that he came to her husband in a dream that week and a phone call to him would confirm this.

Jodie called her husband and he confirmed that Vince had indeed come into his dream and told him horse Number 3 would win the big race. Apparently, in a reading some years ago, Vince told Jodie and her sister that one day he would prove to her husband that he was around him as he loved him like a son. Without the horse race even beginning, Vince had now proven he was around – Jodie's husband hadn't shared the details of the dream with anyone.

The following week, I shared the story with the healing group and discovered that someone else's loved one had also given a prediction in a dream for the same horse race but different numbers. I was now excited as I knew that Team Spirit had set up the whole scenario for teaching purposes. I explained to the group that on this side of life, Vince lived life to the full and knew the horse racing industry very well – he was just about a bookie himself. They had chosen a pretty good candidate for teaching purposes and I shared with the group my doubts and limitations of his ability to predict with total accuracy the outcome of the big racing event.

Some of the members of the group didn't worry too much about the teaching in it all and were backing up Vince's prediction. Vince was now invincible and the group was confident that horse Number 3 would be first over the finishing line. I warned them of the doubts I had and that there would be greater learning in it all. They seemed to be caught up in the fun of what Vince may be able to offer. It was harmless at the time and I'm sure Team Spirit and Vince were laughing at the confidence that everyone had in him.

The evening before the big race, Team Spirit asked me to sit down with a notepad. They provided three statements in a riddle format that made no sense to me at all and I wrote them down. Upon completing this, they advised me that they were the winning horses, in order, for the next day and upon looking at the racing guide it would be clear who they were. I obtained a copy of the newspaper and I was excited to see that it was evident who the horses were – and the numbers didn't match any of those provided by deceased relatives. More importantly than that, I had waited 12 months for answers to my theory on predictions to come to fruition.

The next day, members of the healing group were sending me messages that good old Vince was going to be a star that day. I had not shared my new information with anyone and it was soon confirmed that Team Spirit were indeed correct. The three horses provided by Team Spirit won in the order given. They had proven to me that deceased loved ones have limited ability to predict major events that are not directly attributable to the choices of their loved ones on this side of life.

I believe that when a deceased loved one passes over into the spirit world, they can predict certain events about their living relatives here on earth with a high level of accuracy. It would take a large amount of energy to watch and focus where these choices are heading and in essence a confident prediction can be made. The predictions I'm currently talking about are not the major life-changing events that I believe are concrete in our life contracts. Certain things, such as when we cross over, who we will marry and what our occupation will be are certainly definite forks in the road that do not require much effort to see from the spirit world. I believe these choices were already made before we were born and so it's easy for deceased relatives to know this information without error.

It is the predictions of the choices of how to get to these forks in the road that can change. If someone was meant to meet their husband at a dance and showed no interest or walked straight past them, their meeting would be attempted again but perhaps in another environment. Either way, the major forks in the road will be crossed eventually and there can be different options or paths that can be taken to get there. It is the prediction of these complicated dirt roads or paths that can be extremely difficult, especially when there are so many players involved making decisions and choices all the time. This is why concrete predictions by loved ones cannot always be made on the dirt paths that are paved in an attempt to get to the fork in the road. So much energy would be required to predict these with total accuracy.

This brings up the whole topic of connectivity between souls. If your deceased loved ones were more evolved beings that were further along the road of awareness, they would be more connected with souls of both the earth plane and spirit world. They could therefore predict much further with accuracy than the average soul, since they're connected to souls outside their own loved ones. I believe the reason for this is that through connectivity to one another, the energy flow is no longer disconnected on an individual level and a knowingness of what a person chooses is not separate to oneself.

It's not much different to when people say that God experiences life through his children. God's experience would be the conglomeration of all the choices of all souls. Given that God or the universe is the source of all connectivity, then God or the universe is well aware of all choices made by everyone, so therefore the prediction equates the exact outcome of all choices.

From my understanding of this, I believe that the more evolved the soul is in the spirit world, the greater their ability to make accurate predictions on wider events. The outcome of an event is based on the choices of many people involved. If masses of people were making choices that affect the outcome of one particular event, then the average deceased loved one would find it difficult to attempt to guess all these possible choices made.

This applies to predicting the outcome of a horse event. There are plenty of horses in the race and the choices made on the day extend across to all riders involved. Now if the outcome is not the result of a major concrete fork in the rider's life plan, or the person in the spirit world predicting is not connected to the winner on a deeper soul level, then accurate prediction of the outcome would be extremely difficult for the average deceased loved one.

If, however, a more evolved soul was predicting the outcome of the event, then a prediction could be made with accuracy. Through greater levels of connectivity to the human souls, they are able to already experience the outcome of all the choices made by everyone, since they have an understanding of no separation. Your experience is also their experience and from this a prediction of your choices results in the prediction of the outcome.

Now if my spirit guides can predict these larger events with accuracy, why have I not yet won the lotto or a major horse race? This is a very good question and the answer to this is quite simple. Firstly, these souls have moved further along the evolution path due to the fact that they have disconnected from the material temptations of the earth plane. The only reason they draw close to the earth plane is to provide healing to humanity or teaching on a mass level. If the prediction doesn't serve the purpose of healing or teaching, then my spirit guides are not interested in providing it at all.

Secondly, I also believe that there are certain universal laws as these souls progress further that do not permit such information to be given to the medium. The purpose of my guides is to provide me with information that will assist in healing or teaching. They are not there to serve my material world needs and I have a complete understanding and respect for this on all levels. Anyone asking for this sort of information from the spirit world would not be a candidate to work with them anyway. Such a soul still connected to the needs and wants of the earth plane of existence is not prioritising the evolution of the human race and that is the sole purpose of mediumship.

Chapter 17

Everything is Borrowed

A passive approach through patience can open the door much easier than hinging on the bets of others to pull you through.
Team Spirit

Just as your soul enters the earth's atmosphere for the beginning of its journey through connecting to the womb of your mother, it will also leave this way, with nothing but its own consciousness and soul body upon exit of the earth plane through physical death. No physical objects are brought into this world upon birth and no objects of matter can be taken with you when you die. This is a fact that all human beings know and believe to be true. The physical body you currently reside in is also borrowed and will return to the earth once its purpose has been fulfilled.

If all human beings know this to be true regardless of race, religion or background, then why do the earth's inhabitants struggle to understand that everything is borrowed for a temporary experience? We are all spiritual beings here for a physical existence and not physical beings residing on earth for an occasional spiritual experience. If everyone in the world does agree that everything here is borrowed, then why does there seem to be very little effort placing this rational thought into practice across widespread humanity?

If we know that everything is borrowed and we own nothing both when we are born and when we physically die, then why is there such a drive to own so much in between? What is the purpose of all this if it is only borrowed for a temporary period of time and it must at one stage be handed over to someone else? Regardless of whether this "someone else" means your relatives, friends or strangers, who's to say that these physical objects are even necessary for those other souls who inherit them for their own temporary soul journey? What purpose do these physical objects play in the evolution of their souls?

Perhaps one of the greatest teachings that the spirit world has ever given to me has been on the subject of the energy exchange of giving and receiving. I struggled with this lesson for a very long time as my over-giving personality found me at times in situations I knew were unhealthy not only for me but also for the work of the spirit world. They used these circumstances as both teachings and examples and continued to do so until I finally raised my hands and surrendered to them one day and said, "*I get the teaching.*"

In my earlier days of demonstrating to audiences, I would spend an additional eight to 10 hours of my time after a normal day of work driving to the events in traffic, setting up the chairs, demonstrating for more than two hours, cleaning up again and then driving home for a few more hours. It would be the early hours of the morning by the time I arrived home, totally exhausted from a Friday evening demonstration but very content about the healing provided that evening from spirit.

With the audiences growing in size very quickly and limited seating for everyone, a small donation fee was no longer covering the cost of the premises and the additional requirements of running these large events. People were also arriving late to the events and banging on the closed doors, even though we had clearly stated that the doors had to be locked down for energy reasons at a specific time. They were now even disrespecting the rules that were clearly outlined by spirit and even placed empty envelopes in the donation boxes as they walked through the doors.

As loved ones' readings were being interrupted by those not respecting both my work and that of spirit, my guides began to step in to teach me some valuable lessons. One evening, I heard one of my guides clearly state: *"There is no time in our world, Louise, and we are all here on time. We expect the same from your world."* I know it takes a lot of energy for my team and your loved ones to come and draw close to the earth plane to connect with me on platform and it takes a lot of energy from me, too.

When someone is late or interrupts, it holds up this energy, making us use more of our limited battery capacity to work with spirit. A distraction can also cause a temporary disconnection with the spirit which can then take away the healing message provided in a loved one's reading.

I soon began to realise the importance of energy exchange with my guides. They didn't *have* to be there at platform. They had *chosen* to come and assist people in need and it would exhaust them to a certain degree, just like it did to me. I didn't realise before that being interrupted was disrespectful to my guides as well as the other spirits – it was through these unfortunate situations that I began to listen to the greater learning and teaching they presented to me.

Before starting an event, I always check the clocks to ensure they are precise when making the decision to close the doors. This ensures that everyone is treated fairly upon arrival. Once the doors are locked down, no entry is permitted. One evening my volunteers and I double-checked both clocks in the room and everything seemed to be perfect. The doors were closed and the evening ran beautifully with some wonderful messages from the spirit world.

When I arrived home, very exhausted but on that natural high after platform, my guides prompted me to check my mediumship phone. It was the early hours of the morning and I was shocked to hear the most terrible message from an abusive lady. This is very rare but the lady had called many times that week and I had tried to explain to her that the events are for healing and not for material self-gain messages. She had attempted to come through the doors that evening and they were locked but she insisted she was there two minutes before the close-off time.

I asked my guides if this was true and their reply was that they had physically changed the clocks themselves. I was completely shocked and they advised that the lady was not arriving for the greater good of everyone in the room or healing and would disrupt the evening for her own self-gain regarding obtaining knowledge on her next home. She had many lessons to learn in this life on giving and receiving and my guides advised me to call her the next day with this information. Upon calling her, my team guided my words with love and to my surprise I know the healing was a great turning point in this woman's life. Through truth and self-reflection from spirit, a message she had needed and not wanted was given to her in the timing that would not affect the greater healing of the audience the night before.

The irony of this lady being locked out was that there was an extreme giver at the door at the same time. He stopped the lady from damaging the door and told her he believed she was being selfish and unfair to spirit's work. He left after the incident, without entry himself. My guides advised me to track him down as he had come to receive some healing for his wife that evening. As a gift from spirit, they advised me to invite him for some personal physical healing at the healing group. He had served and respected spirit and in return they would provide him and his wife with hands-on spiritual healing. They would not have received hands-on healing at the event, so the energy exchange with spirit was more than beneficial for all involved.

This greater teaching of giving and receiving has been demonstrated through my audiences time and time again. Team Spirit will take every opportunity to teach their principles and on one evening they even surprised me. I was almost ready to close down the doors when they prompted me to wait a few moments. As I waited, I could only imagine what they had in mind. No, they didn't change the clocks, so please don't use that excuse at any of my events in the future. Changing the clocks was a one-off teaching incident!

Within a few minutes, a man was staggering through the back doors and looking for a place to sit. There were hardly any chairs and the audience began to talk a lot. He looked homeless and his clothing was torn and dirty. He had the biggest blue eyes I had ever seen and I asked him to find a seat and make himself at home. He soon found a seat and as he sat on the white chair cover, his dirt began to drip on the floor. I could see in everyone's faces how uncomfortable they were while he was in the room.

The first reading was a man in spirit who had taken his life while down and out. The evidence was great and the healing to the family was immense. The spirit had provided insight that appearances are not always what they seem and holding up these appearances can take their toll on anyone. What was to come next was the powerful teaching provided by spirit. As I channelled through a message at the end of platform from my guides on giving and receiving, there was greater learning on the exchange of energy to one another on a universal level, without judgement. The man who had walked into the room earlier on was a prime example of this. He had old and dirty clothing on but underneath this material clothing was a soul that was equal to every other spirit in the room.

Spirit advised me after that evening that a door fee needed to be placed on the events. This took a lot of adjustment for me – in fact it took many months before I finally surrendered and executed their request. They had mentioned to me on a number of occasions that I had a belief that needed to be removed, just like any physical world belief. This belief was preventing the events from expanding and the healing of the spirit world had to be taken to the greater masses.

One morning they woke me and clearly said: *"Louise, great spiritual leaders such as the Dalai Lama charge for their events. They understand the value of energy exchange. Only when there is an exchange of energy is there value and gratitude. Only when there is gratitude, the wisdom of the spirit world will be heard."* Thousands of years ago, if a Native American chief wanted to provide wisdom to someone, he did not simply give the information as it would fall on deaf ears. He may have directed the person to wander for days to find a certain bird feather. Then once he arrived at the chief's tent and presented the feather, he would listen to every word given and the wisdom would be taken with gratitude. It's only when there's gratitude that something can be valued in the exchange process. This is an important part of the universal law of giving and receiving.

I soon realised I wasn't teaching this important universal law to humanity. I was over-giving and the exchange was way out of balance. This meant that at times the gratitude and value among humanity was lost. Money is a form of energy exchange in the physical world and even though my guides were not receiving payment, their work was not valued or received with thanks. I finally got the lesson and began to slowly break down my beliefs on energy exchange.

Everything here in the physical world is borrowed. If an energy exchange of any sort is required along the way to evolve, then that is fine.

This energy exchange must give value to the soul's experience and it is this value that is the most important factor in spiritual growth. The initial reason for arriving for an earthly experience is to grow and connect with greater humanity. This can only be done through practising the universal principles of giving and receiving.

Of all the material wealth spent in one's life here on earth, exchanges of energy along the way to value certain soul experiences are very important. Doctors save physical lives and an exchange of energy in the form of a payment is required somewhere along the line for the service provided. If there was no exchange of energy at all for these services, many would abuse the system and not have gratitude towards the work of the doctor, their own physical bodies or those who have a greater need apart from their own. By placing a value on the service, an awareness is given to the needs of a more connected humanity, which in turn provides teaching for the universal law of giving and receiving.

It has taken the earth plane to arrive at a crisis point for us to start to understand the importance of energy exchange. Most human beings are now aware that recycling of energy is required to live a sustainable life and that Mother Earth cannot continually give without receiving. Every human being has the responsibility to recycle and reuse their energy, with an understanding that both our physical body and the environment we live in is only borrowed for a temporary experience.

Chapter 18

Peace Among the Deceased

A dark well without wishes is like a soul without light.
Team Spirit

I strongly believe that mediumship itself requires a need on either side of the bridge – a need for the spirit to give an important healing message to someone on this side of life, or for someone on the earth plane to have another conversation with their loved one to allow them to move forward in the next journey of their current life. Either way, mediumship requires a need of some sort to make communication, otherwise there would be no purpose in it at all.

A lot of people have the impression that spirits with unfinished business have a higher priority to communicate than those who left their physical life with greater levels of peace. This is not always the case. I believe that healing can stem from many sources. Someone who has left the earth plane with no unfinished business can provide a powerful, loving reading to the audience that can also be an effective teaching tool from the spirit world's perspective. Mediumship can be very powerful for an audience when those communicating in spirit can leave healing messages with everyone and not just their loved ones being read.

I know that when the spirits come forward and start blending their energy with me, there can at times be a level of hesitation or nervousness, so to speak, on their part. They may be frightened that the person in the audience will not own up to them, or that perhaps I won't understand exactly what they're saying, or they may be seeking some form of closure on something that was left behind unresolved. I always encourage them and let them know that we'll do fine together and it's this trust and inner peace within me that also helps bring peace among the deceased.

I strongly believe there is a direct correlation between the peace of those residing in the spirit world and the peace of loved ones here on earth. On so many occasions, the messages can be very comforting for those receiving them just at the time they need to hear them most. They are comforted by a knowingness that they're not facing their lives here on earth alone and deceased relatives on the other side are always near to guide and assist wherever possible.

My old housemate Simone didn't receive many messages from the spirit world in the few years we lived together as I believe there wasn't a great need for healing. On one occasion after finishing platform, a little girl in spirit who wanted to get a message to her brother who lived interstate woke me in the middle of the night. Her brother was feeling very guilty over the passing of his sister in a tragic accident. She was keen for me to speak to Simone to contact her mother to pass the message on. Simone knew the family very well. The next day, Simone called interstate and the visitation and evidence was soon confirmed. The timing of the visitation couldn't have been better and the healing was definitely required.

Only recently, I contacted Simone again regarding a lady in spirit who had been interrupting my dreams nightly with a sense of urgency. I could never see her but her voice was very clear and she kept talking about the children and wanting to speak to her daughter. She clearly identified who her daughter was and after a couple of nights the information was confirmed. Simone's friend was getting married the following week and her friend's sister-in-law was pregnant. I asked Simone to speak to her friend immediately and ensure the two ladies acknowledged the visitation from their mother figure. Once they acknowledged this it would provide their mother with an immense amount of peace – and me as well with the phone line down and a good night's sleep!

On so many occasions, I've seen the spirits showing me their loved ones praying to them at night and asking for assistance. I hear what they're asking for and the powerful confirmation that those words were actually heard can be very healing. The outcome of the situation doesn't matter, it only matters that they were heard. I believe this peace through confirmation provides further comfort and resolution to the situation involved.

I will never forget the reading of a blind lady in my audience that moved all of us. She was elderly but full of life and had flown halfway across Australia convinced that her husband in spirit would be meeting her that night at platform. She reminded me so much of my own grandmother, who was also blind but had an incredible faith in what most would consider to be impossible.

Her husband was first off the rank in the readings and his love for his wife was immense. He provided excellent evidence and even clearly stated their pact to meet one another again at platform. He had come to her in a dream and said he would be there and she believed him without question. Call it blind faith but the peace the reading provided to everyone in the room that night was heartfelt on a very deep level. It proved to everyone that love never separates us, even if we can no longer physically see each other.

I remember one evening a vibrant young spirit by the name of Shane arriving at platform. He was totally out there and was a florist who passed at an early age. I immediately blended well with his energy since he was outgoing like me and lived life to the full. He was ready to connect with his mother, Margaret, in the audience but also saw the opportunity to entertain and provide some teaching to everyone else. Margaret had never been to my platforms and she wasn't even supposed to be at the event that night. It seemed, however, that Shane and the spirit world had other plans and she was soon bombarded with her energetic son's communications.

Shane provided lots of evidence to his mother, as well as confirmation that life continued on and he was in a happy and healthy place. There was no judgement where he resided and he even had a few laughs about his funeral moving premises. Shane had me in fits of laughter – and everyone else as well – with his uniqueness providing powerful teaching and healing through humour. Margaret donated a beautiful big amethyst healing crystal for platform on behalf of Shane. This crystal reminds us all that every aspect of ourselves is unique and that healing is a birthright to all souls that make their way over to the spirit world.

The spirit world can also bring forward new friends, companions and family when there is great loss in someone's life, to provide some peace. Briony, who assists with the Newcastle platform events, lost her mother figure to illness some years ago and I know she was sent to us for a reason. Within three weeks of giving birth to her daughter Lily, she also lost her best friend Suzie, who passed away suddenly into the spirit world. Suzie was the godmother of her child and I have no doubt that she is now a major guide in Lily's life, too.

Suzie's mum Deidre now has a grandaughter figure in Lily and together they share an immense soul connection. Briony has become a part of my family, too, with Lily blending in well with all the other children in the family. I know that Suzie has assisted with this guidance from the other side and the love she has for her friends and family is absolutely wonderful.

I have seen Suzie a number of times while setting up for platform, bossing me around on how to pack and unpack the angel trailer. Her humour and strong personality continues to provide peace and comfort to us all. Like most spirits, she is always around providing peace in the knowing that love and life do not end through physical death.

There have been occasions where the spirit world have brought together estranged family members in my audiences. Once the spirit has come through and identified themselves clearly, two people may raise their hands in separate parts of the room to claim they are the loved ones of the spirit. Soon we realise they are all family members and neither party knew the other was coming, since they were estranged. The spirit will then provide comfort and healing to those involved and ask that forgiveness be given of the situation and to resolve their differences. Unfortunately I have seen this many times and a lot of the time it is due to disputes over wills upon the physical death of a loved one.

Discussion of wills is not normally a topic of healing on platform, as the spirit world is no longer interested in physical world material matters. But if the will is causing a lot of pain and grief, then of course these details can be shared if necessary. Most of the time the spirit will ask for fairness and perhaps have seen that either a lack of action or too much action before they passed didn't help the situation either. So far, on all these occasions I have seen the family members coming together again through healing. This is very powerful, as it could have lasted another 50 years on this side of life until healing was finally executed when all family members had passed over.

I know that such a reading provides teaching to the audience members as well. It teaches them to speak their truth about their wishes and, if it's important to them, to ensure those wishes are clearly stated. This prevents a medium having to deal with it when they pass over as well. On a few occasions, I've seen the situation where the requests of the deceased have been overridden causing a little unrest for them in the spirit world. It's not the material aspects of this that affects them so much but the lack of truth that's executed on their behalf.

Most of the spirits don't talk about these aspects of the material world since they have moved beyond those matters. I have had spirits pass over and come through platform before their own funeral. As evidence they have stated the funeral arrangements and have even asked that their outfit in the coffin or the music be changed. I know this humour provides peace and comfort not only to the spirit but to their loved ones as well. I always find these readings fascinating as I believe most spirits attend their own funerals since it gives peace and closure to family members in both worlds.

I know a spirit is at total peace with their passing when they use a lot of humour regarding the cause of their death. I am very mindful of not going too far with it and I trust that the spirit is just bringing forward both evidence and their personalities. I remember a reading once where four men were lost at sea and never returned home. As I was communicating with their loved ones in the audience, the four of them were laughing that their bodies would never be found as they were now fish food.

I was cautious how I communicated this information in the reading and it was soon evident that this was exactly what they would have said on this side of life. The humour provided lots of healing to the family and proved that they all survived the traumatic experience and were now at peace, even though their physical remains would never be found.

I cannot count the number of times a spirit will step forward while on platform and provide me with their exact time of death. I will immediately be aware of who was present at the time of their passing and those who simply were not meant to be there. The spirits are well aware of the reasoning behind who should and who should not have been there once they pass over. They're quick to comfort them through the reading on exactly what the person was doing at the time of their passing so they don't feel like they've missed out.

My guides have provided an explanation of why some people are present at the time of passing while others are not. It's just like when doctors attempt to revive someone on this side of life to keep them in this world and the staff around the doctor may ask some of the family members to leave the room. It may be that they're distressed, or causing a distraction to the work that needs to be done. Either way, certain people are escorted out of the room to allow the doctor to do the necessary work.

There's not much difference when the spirit world is attempting to take someone from this world. They, too, have a job to encourage the soul to come with them through the light and into the spirit world for healing. If certain family members are holding a person back, this can make their work much harder when attempting to encourage them to move into their new world through physical death.

This is why so many people pass when someone leaves the room. The spirit world and deceased loved ones see an opportunity to collect those making the transition with as little fuss as possible. Those who are meant to be there at the time of their passing will be there. Those who are not meant to be there may experience obstacles as it's pre-ordained that they're not meant to be physically there.

I have seen spirit providing proof through many readings that they have observed what their loved ones were doing even across the other side of the world at the exact time of their passing. You don't need to be physically there when they pass – no-one ever leaves this world alone or frightened and you're not alone when your loved ones cross over either. We're all connected on a much deeper soul level. This connectivity can never be broken and it is this knowingness among the deceased that truly brings peace to souls on both sides of life.

There are no doubt times when even I am surprised at the power of the spirit world to bring forward peace. Some of the readings in the audiences are not directly for people who have lost loved ones as immediate family members. Many people receive readings with communication from spirits who were neighbours, friends of friends or even distant relatives or work colleagues. It doesn't matter, since the person in the audience has also been chosen to be the medium or messenger between the two worlds.

Normally when a spirit comes through the platform who is not directly related to the recipient in the audience, I still ask the spirit for specific evidence. Apart from clearly identifying themselves, they will also bring forward accurate observations from the spirit world that they have observed of the person in the audience. The audience member most often wonders why a spirit of such distant relationship knows their personal details.

The reason for this is that they wish to provide even more proof of their existence so the recipient of the message builds up the confidence to pass it on to their loved ones. Most of the time the spirit world will use any means of getting a message to their loved ones, even if this involves using another channel apart from the medium. It makes sense – there are millions of souls wishing to contact their loved ones and fewer mediums in the physical world to make the contact. So using a second messenger will be necessary at times.

Upon completing a reading, I often find that the spirits want to give me details of what they're up to in the spirit world. It's so easy for grief to leave people in a state of shock to the extent where they don't think about the new life of the spirit. Death can bring about selfish feelings in a person and sometimes those feelings and thoughts are not peaceful to either the spirit or the loved ones left behind.

Most people ask themselves questions like: What am I going to do without you? Who is going to look after me? What about the debts you left behind? Why did you go before your time? It's only when the emotion settles down through the stages of grief that insight and peace can be restored. Through understanding that certain events and incidents shape who we are in life, we are then able to grow into the people we are today.

My guides have brought to my attention that not many people ask the spirits about their new life on the other side. When a person dies through physical illness, those left behind see only the suffering and not the relief that's restored for those souls through physical death. All souls continue life in another place with new interests and meeting up with wonderful family and friends. They have a new start and have so much to share with their loved ones apart from physical death.

Many ask the spirits for help with issues on this side of life. It would be nice every now and then to send them loving and positive thoughts for their new life in the spirit world. They are not in any pain or suffering, it is only those who are left behind who are subjected to this. Let them know that you wish for them to be happy with their new life and that one day you will meet again and share all the experiences they've had since their physical departure from here.

Your peace is also their peace, so start to open your heart and mind to their new life and know within every part of you that one day your lives will be reunited. In the meantime, talk to them and ask for assistance in your life and try to support them in their new life, too. They will come to you in dreams, emotions and feelings and from this subtle contact you'll know that peace among the deceased in the spirit world can also be felt here on earth.

Chapter 19

Journeys to the Other Side

Allow yourselves to shine so far that a shadow of doubt will never follow you.
Team Spirit

I was woken up at 3.45am with a sudden rush of energy. I was wide-awake and could feel my ears, spine and back expand with energy until a clear voice spoke to me. The voice was unrecognisable – definitely not one of my spirit guides. He was very humorous and told me I was about to embark on a learning journey of great teaching. The love and humour from his voice was very relaxing and in time I became aware of a young boy in spirit who hugged me with intense love.

As I flew out of my body at a fast rate, I was aware of everything around me. There were spirit doctors working with my body and they made themselves known to me so I would relax and go on with the voice. I could never see the man whose voice spoke to me and he made me feel very comfortable and so full of love as he took me on this journey.

I was soon in an area that looked like a transitory train station, with people coming and going. I became aware of my grandmother, my brother Andrew and others who had passed over. Strangely enough, it felt like no time had passed at all since I had seen them last and I was happy to leave them after such a short encounter. It surprises me even today that there was no level of hesitation to leave them, as the human side of me would of wanted to stay and catch up some more.

The man's voice stayed with me the whole time and after speaking to my loved ones on the other side, I told him that no-one would believe I had been there. He said to me I could ask for any spirit that I had never met in life, and he would bring this person forward as evidence that the visitation to the spirit world was real. I mentioned that a friend of mine who was also a medium had lost a brother to suicide years before and that she missed him dearly. I didn't know his name and in no time this man stepped forward and introduced himself as Alan.

Alan looked at me with a grin. He had sandy coloured hair, facial hair and a distinctive tattoo on his arm. He was riding a skateboard and had a little message at the back of it: *"Love is the way."* He had a little poster with him as well, promoting his sister's services in the spirit world. The poster had plenty of spelling mistakes on it and later I learnt that he was dyslexic in life – he had used good humour as evidence. The voice then asked me to board a train and Alan rode his skateboard beside me, laughing as he disappeared.

I was then standing in a beautiful city and everything seemed very large around me. I rose into the air and could look over boats full of people coming into the spirit world. I asked why the people were on boats and the spirit world replied. They said that if the souls had loved the water in life, then they would be brought into the spirit world in an environment suited to their personalities so there would not be too much adjusting while they were going through their transitional healing phase.

The people on the boats looked so peaceful as they caught up with their loved ones in such a beautiful environment. I'm sure most of them never had the chance to do so on the earth plane. This part of the journey was no doubt the most enjoyable. The landscape was evergreen and much light penetrated through my body as I flew around the cities meeting many people along the way.

I was quickly taken to a reception area where a lady stepped forward and said to me that I needed to stop asking so many questions and just enjoy the journey. She said this would be one of many journeys and one day I would write about these journeys in books. For now, she said, enjoy the experience and there would be plenty of time to talk later. She said they were excited in the spirit world that I could adjust to the vibrations so quickly and travel through the various planes of existences with ease.

The lady then went on to explain to me that they had thought these journeys of such intense shifts in energy would only be possible in a place known as Tibet on earth. This place has crossover points to the spirit world that allow the spirit doctors to adjust the frequency of the body a little easier. They were celebrating that I had arrived okay and could hear and see very clearly with no impact on the physical body left behind on the earth plane.

I remember meeting a man in a homeless shelter. As I stopped and turned back, I asked the people around him why there was such a hut in the spirit world. One man told me that the man had just passed over and given that he was homeless on the earth plane, it was best they placed him in an area he felt comfortable with while they explained to him that he had physically died. They said they attempt to put people in an environment that's similar to where they were on the earth plane if they know it will make them more at ease throughout the transition process of physical death.

As I began to descend on my way back to the earth plane, I became very aware of a pull towards a heavy physical body in a negative atmosphere. It felt like I had lots of wet clothing on in an environment that seemed very smothering and foggy. Once the voice left me I woke up, totally aware of everything and checked the time. It was 6.30am so I had been gone for almost three hours. As I quickly started to write everything down, I had already begun to miss the voice and the peaceful places I had visited. Every part of me wanted to go back and I realised this would not occur in my own time.

While I was on the other side, the spirit world said it would become evident why I had been shown the transitory area and the many other places. Only some hours before, one of my sister's best friends passed suddenly of heart failure and would have been making her way through transition. I know I wasn't meant to meet Suzie right then in the spirit world – perhaps it would have been too much of a surprise for the two of us. But when I shared this story with my little sister Barbs that morning, I know it brought some comfort to know that Suzie was in a peaceful place that was suited to her personality, with plenty of helpers and loved ones.

I contacted Alan's sister Kerrie and she validated all the information. He even gave a little prediction that came true for Kerrie some months later. I know that I chose to meet Alan for a few reasons on a deeper level. I know that my heart wanted to provide some healing for Kerrie and I also know now more than anything that everyone ends up in the same place in the spirit world regardless of how they pass over, including suicide. This was the greater teaching for me to give to many souls that needed to know this answer.

As for Alan's message, "Love is the way," a friend sent an email that morning titled exactly that: "Love is the way," and she had no idea where I had been that morning. It was powerful confirmation of my visitation to the spirit world and once again re-enforcing the important healing message that love is the only way and it can never separate us – not even through physical death.

Throughout the years, I have been to the spirit world on many occasions. I have never met another medium who has been over like that before, so I see it as a great privilege and something that needs to be shared as spirit has advised. On every occasion I have visited, I haven't been back to the same place twice – except for my grandmother's house, which I visit all the time on my way through. Even when I go there, I seem to always enter her house differently as there are so many different aspects of her home.

My grandmother loved both Germany and Australia and so her house in the spirit world is partly her old unit in Germany and partly our former family home in Australia. I know this sounds strange but it's true. She has created a home in the spirit world that reminds her of her best memories here on the earth plane. My stepbrother Tony, who passed away suddenly some years ago, also confirmed this to me through his crazy idea of taking me over to his house one evening.

My father had just married Helga. A week after the wedding, Helga's son Tony decided to drop in and visit me. He woke me up in the middle of the night and with his cheeky good looks, told me there was a place he wanted to show me. I felt my body relax and I walked out of it. I walked through my bedroom door and flew with Tony at a very high speed. He was a risk-taker in life, so every part of me knew he was going to push the boundaries.

I remember clearly going through a tunnel and landing at a particular house. The number of the house was 42 and it had a distinguished zigzagging hallway. He then opened the door of a bedroom and also showed me other areas of the house. It was a maze and he then said he wanted to show me different parts of the universe. I told him I thought I had been gone too long and wanted to go back in case I never returned. He reassured me that my guides had everything under control and he laughed as we flew around different places with such excitement. We were like small children, even though we were adults.

Upon returning to my body, I quickly documented everything and called Helga. She confirmed that indeed they had lived in such a house when Tony was a child many years before – in number 42 with the exact zigzagged hallway I described. She also confirmed the layout of his bedroom and the items around the room I clearly saw. This was Tony's little house in the spirit world and I had been there. I found it to be pretty cool and I know he did, too – the experience no doubt shared some great memories of his life here on earth and some powerful teaching as well. I had never met Tony on this side of life and I know that if we had met we would have got along very well. I could see so much of myself in his vibrant energy.

I have found from my visitations to the other side a constant theme of loved ones creating an environment for their new life that is of heartfelt importance. On the earth plane, human beings struggle all their lives to create homes of value in wealth either for financial security or inheritance purposes. Either way, it doesn't seem to match what they end up creating in the spirit world if there was no deep emotional connection to that environment. I suppose this brings forward the meaning of a difference between a house and a home. The spirit world only has homes, as these are merely created through memories of love and not financial gain. Material gain is only a characteristic of existence on the earth plane.

When he was just four years of age, my brother-in-law David lost his father through a sudden heart attack. I had never seen his father in spirit and we hardly ever spoke of him. I had known David for more than 15 years and sometimes I wondered if I'd cross paths with his father. One evening I was at a healing session, when all of a sudden I was asleep and floating in the spirit world. A man stepped forward and was very excited to see me. He said his name was Patrick and he was David's dad and the love he sent through my body to take back to everyone was intense.

I could clearly see an old vehicle in front of me and he wrote up his full name and location on the door of the vehicle. He was wearing a singlet, smiling with a sense of youth and wanted to show me around his property. He wasn't the man I expected. He was youthful and the same age as when he passed, which was David's current age. I suppose sometimes we expect to meet someone and they end up being a lot different than we thought. I always thought of him as a father figure and not a youthful, hard-working man who was proud of his property and had a great sense of humour.

The next day I contacted David and his two sisters Roslyn and Diane. They confirmed the information and that the property was one he had been connected with many years ago. Obviously he was very happy there. They also confirmed that a big family reunion would be occurring on that property some weeks later, which was further validation. The visitation had emphasised the importance that spirit encounters will be on their timing and once again in an atmosphere that is more suited to them rather than us.

Not long after this visitation I had an almost identical one. My housemate Sonja had lost her father some years ago. I had never met him and knew very little about him. One evening I left my body and found myself in his little heaven. His hair had white and grey through it and he had on very distinctive brown clothing that grabbed my attention and was validated soon afterwards. He was very happy to have me there and when he asked me to sit down he was beaming with excitement. He said that he had found peace in the spirit world and was helping lots of people.

He kept telling me to tell Sonja about "Mueller" and extra days would be added to her trip near the beach. The next day Sonja received an automatic email from someone by the name of "Mueller" and two days were added to her trip to India near the beach. This further validated that I had been with her father in the spirit world and it confirmed once again that nothing can ever tear us apart – not even the distance between two worlds.

It is hard to explain the loss of time that I experience when I visit the spirit world. I know that just before I'm ready to leave, I stay awake for a couple of minutes and feel a gradual pull from my body before moving through a tunnel. I'm normally woken up around 3.30 or 3.45am and arrive back between 6 and 6.30am. Even though I go for around three hours and I'm totally conscious of everything, I find it difficult to fully document most of the things I see and experience.

Differences in colours, ways of communicating through feeling and thought, as well as their different ways of life are barriers between the two worlds that prevent me from sharing many things with you. What I can say is that there are some very beautiful places that leave emotions in my body for days upon my return to the physical world. This is even difficult to explain in words.

I know that if time could be equated between the two worlds, it would be around 100 years on this side of life to around a few weeks on the other side. This is why it always seems like you haven't missed your loved ones in the spirit world, since a lifetime here is just a drop in the ocean over there. Through visitations to the other side, I have obtained a greater level of understanding of this loss of the concept of time and space which most of us live by so much in the physical world.

Time and space allow us to measure our lives with relativity. They show how far we have progressed on the earth plane through the life cycle of birth, child, adolescence, adult, parenting and even death. We measure major milestones in life by using time and all our interactions with one another rely heavily on these earthly concepts. One concept cannot work without the other. For example, I will meet you at three o'clock at the church, or your flight is scheduled for 6am departing Sydney. Everything here on earth has its time and place.

Just like everything here on earth has a time and place, so does the spirit world. There is a level of knowingness about when it's your time to make transition and when it isn't. If it isn't, they will simply return you to the earth plane with a greater level of understanding of life than you previously had. This is why so many people who have near-death experiences dramatically change their lives when they return after surviving physical death. Something switches inside them and they are never the same again.

When I was around 25 years of age, I became unwell for a period of nine months with problems relating to my heart. I remember one evening going to the spirit world and having no recollection of being there. I love life to the full and anyone who knows me knows I never think of life here on earth as being negative at all. When I returned from there, I never felt so homesick in my life. I had no recollection whatsoever and I wanted to go back. I felt like this for about a week and upon reflection now, I know they removed those memories so I could return to the earth plane focusing on the work that needed to be done here and not wondering what was going on over there.

During the time I was unwell, two of my work colleagues had exactly the same heart condition as me. It was not a coincidence that the three of us had the same diagnosis and perhaps I was the only one who could see the humour in it all. I wasn't a worrier like Jenny and Joanne, especially when the doctors told us our lives could be cut short earlier than most. Jenny passed away a couple of years later and a few years after that Joanne also passed away into spirit. Back then I thought I would go first but obviously that was not the plan of the spirit world.

I clearly remember the shock of receiving the news from Joanne that she had passed away suddenly. I was walking on the beach when she made her presence known and soon this was confirmed in the physical world. It is those moments that bring back so much reflection in your own life regarding the meaning of it all: why we have come here and how all our lives have different purposes. Once these purposes are fulfilled, it is then that we will go home to the spirit world and not beforehand.

Within weeks of receiving the news that Joanne had passed, a lady standing at the end of my bed woke me. I didn't recognise her and when I asked her who she was, she said she was me after I pass over into the spirit world. I had never ever experienced my own spirit projecting to me and I shared the experience with the healing group – with a little humour as well. Why did I need to see and hear that information? Was there something inside me at a deeper level that asked this question and my higher spirit answered it? It was no doubt the strangest spiritual experience I had ever encountered.

A few weeks later I was woken up at around 4.30am. The feeling I had washing over me was very intense and I had never felt like that before. My body was vibrating at a very rapid rate and I felt as though there were two of me. As I walked into the bathroom and put some water on my face, I had an overwhelming sensation to quickly lie down in my room. As I lay down on the bed I felt my other body vibrating very rapidly, which I knew was my spirit body disconnecting from my physical body.

All of a sudden I was standing outside my body and aware of a valley through my wall. I had never experienced this before – normally I would just disconnect from the physical body and move into the spirit world very quickly. My body felt very different this time and I was consciously aware of some buildings in front of me. I walked through a valley and into a building that I can best describe as a type of hospital.

As I walked into the place, I was surrounded by a lot of young people who had just died in car accidents and from suicides and illnesses. They were all intrigued as to who I was and some of them directed to me that at least I get to go back. I said to them, *"Of course I'm going back – there's too much work to do."* When I spoke of mediumship they had no idea what it was.

I started to speak passionately about mediumship and connecting with loved ones in the physical world and I was totally surprised they had never heard of it before. I suppose they were young and they had just passed over so many of them wouldn't have known about it on the earth plane anyway. It was quite ironic that I was promoting mediumship in the spirit world and explaining to them how they could connect with their loved ones in the physical world.

I soon became aware of people eating and drinking. This had me totally fascinated as I thought they no longer needed to eat or drink in the spirit world since they didn't have a physical body anymore. I was soon corrected – I found out that while in the transition stages of physical death, the spirits do eat and drink and this assists their new etheric body to adjust to the vibrations. The spirits also need to get used to their new life slowly, so if eating and drinking was a part of their routine on the earth plane it would continue for a little while if it was their request.

Just as I was trying to get my head around the people eating and drinking, I became aware of a television show on display in a waiting area. The show had actors who had passed over many years ago all acting together, with lots of comedy as well. By now, many people were gathering around me as my enthusiasm flowed through like never before. Just like demonstrating to an audience in the physical world, there was an audience in the spirit world now listening to the mechanics of mediumship and the greater healing purpose of the gift.

I was in the prime of my life – not sure if it was my spirit life or physical life – but either way I was more alive than ever. Every part of me was bursting with energy as the spirits listened to the stories. Their faces lit up at the possibility of a medium connecting with their loved ones in the physical world and just like mediumship on this side, it gave them a knowingness and peace that nothing can ever separate our communication with one another, even between the two worlds.

In the middle of one of my talks, I was interrupted and asked to drink a certain substance. I was a little annoyed that I didn't get to finish my speech as they simply told me to go back and tell the world that healing most definitely starts in the spirit body or aura as you may know it. They told me what the substance was and then I was thrown into a dark capsule and sent back to my physical body at high speed. I had very clear memories at that stage of being born into the physical world all over again.

As I awoke, I checked the time and it was 6.30am. I was still annoyed that my talk was interrupted. I documented it all in an email and sent it off to my family and the healing group as soon as I could. I had been to the other side again but this time it was the grandest visitation to date. I was convinced that the visitation that morning was a work assignment, to teach those on the other side about mediumship and I was no longer going over just as a guest. I always knew that my work provided healing on both sides of the veil and this time I was consciously aware of it all from the viewpoint of the other side.

Within 24 hours, I walked into the normal fortnightly healing group session eager to personally share my experience with them. I had documented the visitation the day before in an email. But before I had the chance to speak, I felt a sudden pain in my chest and found it difficult to breathe. The healers gathered around me and sent me off to hospital and soon blood tests and scans were underway. I felt an overwhelming sense of calmness when I arrived and the hospital visitation seemed all too familiar from the morning before in the spirit world.

At this stage, I could feel my spirit team placing energy over me and I could breathe normally again. My blood tests had indicated that there was possible clotting in the lungs and they would start anti-clotting treatment straight away. They were convinced that something would be picked up in the scans to match this but there was nothing there at all. I was feeling fine and I could hear the words again: *"Tell the world that healing starts in the spirit body and then moves through the physical body."*

I have no doubt from all my experience with mediumship that I was sent to the spirit world the morning beforehand as a patient and not a visitor. I know that the fast frequency I was feeling and total disconnection from my physical body was necessary for whatever healing they would be conducting on my spirit body in the spirit world. Never before had my body been totally disconnected and vibrating so fast, which is exactly what the spirit body does when disconnecting from the physical body through death.

I know that the spirit world could see a potential problem in my physical body and decided to take me over through total disconnection of the spirit body to conduct some form of healing. Again, the timing of their work was unbelievable as the healing moved from the spirit body to the physical body the moment I walked into the healing group. They used the energy of the healers to execute their work and in no time I was on my way to breathing normally again.

The healing group researched the substance they provided to me in a drink in the spirit world. It was a very strong antioxidant that's used for anti-ageing here on earth and can only be used here in very small dosages. It makes sense that the spirit world used this substance for healing of the spirit body, as the spirit body is timeless and seems never to age. I know that when spirits project themselves to me their body is a replica of their physical body but in a time when the physical body was in the prime of its life.

I have decided not to share with you the substance in the drink as I am not a doctor and it needs to be taken with care. I did not take this substance in this world and if the spirit world wanted me to disclose this, they would have requested for me to do so. It has definitely made me rethink the importance of the connection between the spirit body or aura and the physical body and how they are very much dependent upon one another.

The spirit world is a mental world, so therefore if everything begins with thought then of course it must be created in the spirit body first before manifesting into the physical body. It makes total sense then that healing begins with looking after your thoughts and energy fields and from this manifestation begins in the physical body. I don't need to know all the medical details of what happened that night in the hospital on the other side; I only need to see the learning in it all.

The learning is that there is another world. I've been there enough times to experience it, document it, bring back evidence and then teach it as requested by the spirit world. I don't need approval from others that they have taken me there or that it even exists. The spirit world to me is much more real than this world. It is a place of love, truth and total connection. I hope one day that love, truth and total connection can also be felt on this side of life when the earth plane becomes a more peaceful and enjoyable place for all its inhabitants to exist.

Chapter 20

Signals and Signposts

Why second guess when you have first instincts?
Team Spirit

As I drove home in the rain this afternoon after leaving the intensive care unit of the hospital, every part of me could see the greater learning I had been given today, as well as the learning to come to the readers. I was at exactly the same hospital as the previous chapter and this time for totally different reasons. As a medium, my insights have changed to another level again and I see more clearly now than ever before how much of our lives are comprised of major signals and signposts.

Marisia is a very dear friend and part of the healing group, too. Her husband Phillip had a work accident yesterday – he fell from a ladder, which resulted in a major brain injury. As they rushed him to hospital unconscious, the doctors sedated him and placed him on life support. Today after I arrived at the hospital and spent some time with Marisia and Phillip, the doctors advised that the machines would need to be turned off so Phillip could pass away peacefully.

Throughout the day I had clear flashbacks of how we all ended up in this room together dealing with this very tough situation. More than two months ago, Marisia and I had scheduled a barbecue for today so I could formally meet Phillip. I had seen him in the car when he had dropped off Marisia's father for healing but I hadn't had the chance to spend time with him personally. Given that my schedule is very busy – and I am sure Phillip's was as well – today was the day I decided some months ago that we would eventually get to spend some quality time together.

When I walked into the hospital this morning, I could see that Phillip and I were meant to meet today as scheduled and spend some time together both physically and spiritually. The barbecue was to be an event where Phillip would obtain an insight into the healing group and mediumship and connecting with the other side. As I sat near his bed and held his hand, every part of me knew that this discussion would never have occurred at a barbecue. Our meeting at the hospital would incorporate all of this and much more on a deeper spiritual level in preparation for his new life in the spirit world.

Before the doctors arrived with the news, I sat with Marisia and Phillip and totally trusted in any decision that would be made. Throughout the night I could hear the song *Fields of Gold* and as I watched Phillip's face I knew that was exactly where he was. I knew that by physically meeting him under these circumstances we had both obtained a new level of understanding. We knew at a very deep spiritual level that a major signpost had been arrived at and a new journey would begin shortly. Our meeting would serve a far greater purpose and provide healing to many others from this new understanding.

Once I understood that Phillip had arrived at a signpost, the flashes of the signals upon that arrival were now evident. Yesterday I had organised an electrician to come in and change a light and it was at the exact same time and in similar circumstances that the accident had occurred with Phillip. Phillip was working on a sensor light at the time. At this same time, I was also completing the previous chapter of this book whereby I wrote about Patrick, who I met on the other side, who shares the same last name and regional location as Phillip. Their names also both start with the letter P. Phillip was now in exactly the same hospital that I was writing about at the same time and again the chapter was coming to life under different circumstances. This connectivity has now occurred in three chapters of this book for greater teaching purposes.

You may call it coincidence but for me I see these events as signals. I see them as signals from that higher part of our soul that knows the map of our lives and the direction it must lead. I know that my spirit guides were well aware of this to the extent that today was scheduled with accuracy. I know that Phillip had pre-ordained these events as part of his own life contract for greater learning and soul evolution to occur. This learning would occur for both him and for those who had been left behind on the earth plane.

Many of you may wonder whether my spirit guides had an opportunity to allow me to intervene in the circumstances. That I believe to be very true and there are two major reasons why universal law would never permit this. Firstly, Phillip had chosen this life experience for some reason to evolve his soul and others. What right would my spirit guides have to take this away from his free will and choice? The learning he will leave behind will be a gift, despite all the pain and suffering that's necessary for this soul evolution.

Secondly, if this universal law had been broken and Phillip survived the circumstances, it would have had a snowball effect on everyone else's contracts that are involved. They would not obtain the necessary learning from this physical world exit set up by Phillip in his life contract. Upon eventual return of all the life players to the spirit world, there would be great disappointment for all involved. They would realise that they may need to come back to the earth plane in another incarnation to learn through the same experience again. I'm sure this would bring about great disappointment to everyone involved, especially Phillip's soul.

I believe that these signals and signposts are evident among us each and every day. Sometimes not all the cards can be revealed so that the human side of us does not attempt to intervene and prevent certain necessary events from occurring. Marisia had wanted Phillip to stay home that day and help with the barbecue. Their daughter Katiana would normally have gone to work with him on that particular day but she decided to sleep in. I believe it is the higher self, the soul of Phillip that was communicating with the higher selves of Marisia and Katiana not to intervene. He was preparing for his own exit and from this his soul saw it as a gift and not a sacrifice of physical life.

Natacha is Marisia and Phillip's other daughter and her boyfriend of some weeks had not had the chance to meet Phillip before the accident. When he arrived at the hospital, he realised that some years before his sister had been in the same hospital, the same ward and the same bed as Phillip for a major brain operation. She had only had a five per cent chance of success and she managed to recover and lead a normal life. Was it a coincidence that Phillip ended up in exactly the same place, under similar circumstances but of course with a very different outcome? We both met Phillip in the hospital for the first time and I have no doubt it was an important part of both our life contracts for either teaching or soul growth purposes.

Once loved ones arrive in the spirit world, these signals and signposts continue to be a major part of the lives of those who are left behind. The physical exit of a person sets up new directions in the life contracts of the remaining players. Suddenly, people are more aware of little things that happen around them that seem to be a little more than just coincidences. These little signs can indicate being on course in their own life contracts, or are messages from their loved ones. The signs have always been there but they had not previously taken the time to be aware of them.

I believe that the greatest messages come through other people who are also living on the earth plane. How many times have you had a problem, a question, or needed to make a decision and then someone you have never met answers it for you without consciously being aware of doing so? You may be deciding which company to work for in choosing between two jobs and you find out that someone standing next to you in a coffee queue also works for them or starts talking about them. Most people say, *"Wow, that must be a sign!"* and it most definitely is. There's no such thing as coincidence.

Every soul is linked together through a universal web, each experiencing life through the life of others. None of us can ever live alone and all of us rely heavily on the services of others. The butcher, baker, banker and even the rubbish truck driver are all necessary players in our physical life, so why would they not be important players on a spiritual level? To separate the two would not make sense, for it would make the physical existence senseless.

I believe that many opportunities in life are missed since a lot of people just don't see the signs. It is as though they are waiting for the signpost to hit them directly in the head before they decide to read it. The person may also rely too much on the eyesight of others to read the signs for them and of course each of us will have a different perspective on what it reads. Those reading the signs for you may also be colourblind due to their filtering of past experiences. This would result in them telling you that the light is red when indeed it is flashing green in your life contract.

Perhaps many may perceive me to be strong willed and very persistent. That is very true, and mostly my character is one who doesn't seek the approval or opinion of others very often. I read the signs in my own physical life contract from my higher self, those signs from my spirit guides in the work that I do and of course from your loved ones as well when passing on a message from the spirit world. Knowing the difference between the signs is important and attempting to interpret them correctly without putting too much thought into it is of significance as well. I always trust that in the short term the message may not be evident but in the long run it will come to fruition at the right timing.

I believe timing is of great importance when looking out for signals and signposts in your life. Major signposts throughout your life contract will arise with precise timing and some of the signals you may have missed along the way will perhaps resurface again when you're ready to receive them. It may take three people to walk up to you in the same day and talk about a job before you take action and accept it as a new directional sign in your life.

I know from so many readings that loved ones give signals well and truly before they even arrive at platform that they are coming with a message. Some may not even come through for a reading, but a piece of information in someone else's reading or even the playing of music is enough validation that their sign from a loved one has been real. People will also sit randomly near another person and that person may have exactly the same name, circumstances, events and passing of a loved one as them. I hear about this all the time and it can be powerful healing to those involved, including the spirit.

I remember one evening a young man in spirit coming through the platform who'd passed in a plane crash. He told me straight away that his mate, who he identified clearly by name, originally cancelled on him for the platform event. He provided some great evidence that his friends in the audience were speaking earlier on about Shakespeare and further named another best mate who was not present. He went on with some very specific details and upon waiting for a response from the audience, a group of young men raised their hands and claimed the spirit man.

His friend in the audience did indeed cancel on the spirit but at the last minute changed his mind and decided to come to the event. I believe that the higher part of the man in the audience and the spirit communicated with one another at a soul level. This activation of the signal was so strong that both players came together again and had the chance to communicate with one another in a wonderful and humourous way. It is this listening to the signals that brings the people forward to me before any spirit communication even occurs on platform.

Your loved ones communicate with you each and every day from the spirit world and a lot of the signs get missed. These signs are not grand billboards that will flash in your room with a message. Well, I have actually had those, too, but that's an exception from my spirit guides. These signs are very subtle and when you recognise and acknowledge them, another one will normally come soon after to add to the information or validate it. When Phillip's relatives came down to see him, the coffee cups had spun twice without anyone touching them. This was no doubt a sign that his sister and mother in the spirit world were making themselves known to the family.

Phillip's family were facing an enormous amount of grief already at that moment as they had lost quite a few family and friends in the previous six months including Phillip's sister only a few months before. It is very common for family members and close friends to cross over into the spirit world not too far apart from one another in timing. My understanding of this is that those players were important to one another in their life learning and the lessons have been completed for them in their contracts. There was nothing left for them to learn here and so their exit was necessary for new learning to begin for those who had been left behind on the earth plane.

Don't be afraid of signs delivering bad news to you. I do not believe in bad news anyway, as things that happen in life are meant to happen regardless of what your thoughts or opinions are. You can never stop the train diverting on major life signposts. Any attempt to derail the train will only result in it sliding into the next station. These passengers would already have been guided to avoid your intervention if the greater plan at hand needed to be executed as part of the life contract. If you attempt to slow down the train it will simply pick up momentum again, perhaps by taking a little shortcut and missing the scenic route. Either way, the arrival and destination points on any journey will always remain unchanged even if some of the stations along the way may have changed.

It is only through the trust of the insight of signals, signposts and certain events that has allowed me to be the medium I am today. Without the loss of my brother Andrew, Grandma, Aunt Kate, Fiona and Eunice, I would not have the level of understanding of death that I have at such a young age. By fighting for my own life at birth and being ill again at 25 years of age, I can now empathise with those who require healing in this sensitive area of life, including those who will also make transition into the spirit world through illness.

The events that have come to life while I have been writing this book had cemented signposts and nothing my spirit guides or I could have done would have changed this. We do not have the right or free will to break such universal laws. I am not God but simply a worker of the divine energy who has been sent to teach these principles to humanity. I have simply been guided to be part of these events to teach you all that so much of our lives are pre-ordained, including when we are born and the leaving time and circumstances of our physical death.

How can I teach light at the end of the tunnel if I have never walked through the tunnel and found my own direction through trust and feeling of the divine? So much of the grief left behind after physical death is full of regret about how the circumstances could have changed if the person did this or that. Nothing could have changed these circumstances at all, not even a medium who has insight and a powerful team of spirit helpers on the other side. These major signposts are so cemented into the earthly ground that we need to respect the reasons why the soul had chosen to exit through this experience. The reasons for most people will not be evident until they themselves cross over into the spirit world and review their own life contract and progression of soul growth.

We are all students and teachers to one another and each and every day we give messages of guidance that help us along the way regarding our life contracts. Your deceased loved ones are very active in this and I know that many of the spirits over the years have expressed to me that they go back to the same person if they acknowledge these signs from them. Some may get upset when close relatives come in dreams of distant relatives who had little to do with them in physical life. The reason spirits do this is that the distant relatives are not only receptive to the messages but they are not afraid to deliver them to those the spirit wishes to contact. If I was a spirit and I knew that a phone line was clear, active and would not be hung up when called, I would certainly keep dialling the same number, knowing the message would get through correctly.

Your loved ones not only use the means of a medium or dreams to communicate with you, they also use very subtle everyday signs to make contact. The most common ones I know are certain songs or shows playing when you switch on the radio or television. They may also guide you to a certain number plate of a car that you will see in a moment when you're thinking of them. Feathers or coins are very common indicators of the presence of your loved ones.

It's not the signs that I believe are of importance but rather the acknowledgment of these signs. Once you recognise a sign, tell your loved ones you know it's from them – then they'll get excited. They know you've answered the phone, you've listened and you won't just hang up on them and put it aside as a coincidence. Even if the message is very subtle it can be extremely powerful, especially when the synchronicity of the sign coincides with the timing of your own thoughts.

On many occasions spirits have spoken of these signs in specific detail as evidence in their readings, especially when the signs were clearly missed. People will contact me down the track and say that many signs are now noticed since the reading. I will reply to them that it has nothing to do with me. I simply validated the presence of their loved ones and now their loved ones in the spirit world are active, knowing that those on this side of life are now open to communication through simple signs.

Over time a little sign language can be developed between the two worlds with your loved ones. When they are drawing close to you, a certain song may play or someone may turn up with a specific hat that reminds you of him or her. The room may suddenly smell of their presence or someone may tell the same silly joke they may have told on this side of life. These signs are around us each and every day and it's very easy to miss them if we're not open to receive them.

Open your hearts and minds to your loved ones and allow them to create their own signage in your life. It is this signature from them that will impress on your own soul that we are all unique and we all have a story to tell. Despite the differences in all our life contracts and the twists and turns of signals and signposts, these stories continue to live on in both worlds. Sometimes they wish for you to know this personally and once again share their life experiences, even if they exist in another world that communicates on a more subtle unspoken level than ours here on earth.

Chapter 21

Team Spirit Speaks

To go within is never to do without.
Team Spirit

You all know by now whom I mean when I speak of Team Spirit. They are my friends, colleagues, helpers and guides in the spirit world who assist me in this life in bringing forward healing messages of love to you in many different forms. Throughout this book, I have mostly focused on messages from deceased loved ones who wish to convey to you that life does indeed go on and we will one day reunite with our relatives and friends on the other side.

But behind this veil of light exists great wisdom and knowledge that must also be shared with humanity. You have all come here for a soul experience, to love and accept yourselves and one another and to enjoy every part of life that's handed to you. You are here to see the gifts of life, no matter how hard it may be at times. All entries and exits into this world serve a greater purpose and each and every soul has the right to love and eternal happiness.

Throughout the years, I have spent a lot of time working with the spirit world on trance mediumship.

I have spent almost as much time in a trance state as consciously working with spirit on a platform in an audience environment. A few nights a week, I dedicate myself to sit with spirit in an altered state of consciousness so they can impress my mind with thoughts of wisdom and knowledge as well as varying degrees of trance healing energy for others.

The trance state is a very relaxing state whereby I surrender my mind to my spirit guides and they place different levels of energy over me so I move into a deeper state of consciousness. The energy placed over my mind feels like an anaesthetic and I will shift into altered states depending on the work they wish to achieve. For healing, it's like a lighter state whereby they will take control of my arms and parts of my mind and I'm sometimes aware of what's occurring through an observation viewpoint. Sometimes I can see into my body when they do this and it still amazes me how the spirit world sees things so differently to the physical eyes of the human body.

The trance inspirational state is much lighter, whereby my words will just flow through my mind and come through in a very consistent flow that doesn't involve me thinking about it at all. My guides are inspiring me as to what to say or write and I use this state quite often when addressing the inspirational speech at my platform events. In terms of writing this book, the chapters have been written in this lighter state, too, and this is why each of them was written in just a couple of hours from start to finish, with no stopping and requiring minimal editing later on.

Throughout the years, I have known that trance mediumship would be a very important part of my life. Since I was very little, I had a fascination with these very deep states of consciousness and only a few years ago I found a book I had when I was very young. It was about physical mediumship, a very rare form of mediumship where the medium is placed into such a deep state of consciousness that the spirit world can manifest themselves in voice, projection and touch to their loved ones on this side of life using the energy field of the medium. Even though I had a great interest in this as a small child, I had no idea that the spirit world would pursue my path along this avenue some years later.

One Friday night platform event held in Sydney, I read for a husband and wife at the back of the room who had lost a son by the name of Steven. The evidence was clear and they acknowledged the information from me with a lovely healing message of love from the spirit world. Later on in the evening they introduced themselves as David and Jean and were keen to discuss the possibilities of me pursuing some physical mediumship with them. David and Jean were from England and part of the original group who had worked with one of the world's leading physical mediums some years ago. Given the rarity of this form of mediumship, I was amazed that they were here in Sydney and wishing to pursue a passion I was so fascinated with as a child.

We agreed that the spirit world had brought us together for a greater reason and now we would leave it up to Team Spirit to guide us if this was to be another path of my work. I asked Team Spirit for some evidence of this possibility, since it's such a rare form of mediumship and would involve immense dedication from all parties involved. Physical mediumship can take up to 20 years of consistent dedication with the spirit world to develop and it involves immense amounts of patience and trust for those chosen to be involved. In the long run the healing would be immense but the road would be very long and testing in between and I was not naive to that fact.

A couple of months later, I had more than received my evidence from the spirit world that I needed to pursue this further. It was exactly three weeks to the day Fiona had passed away when I noticed that I became very tired while sitting on my bed. All I could remember was moving into an altered state of consciousness and being with Fiona. We were laughing and really enjoying one another's company and then I found myself in her relative's house with a heightened state of happiness. Soon I returned back to my body with no idea what we were up to but I knew we had shared some special time together.

I called Therese and she said Fiona's relatives had received a phone call from Fiona. Fiona had left a message on their answering machine. They had heard Fiona's voice and I knew in my heart that it was exactly what the two of us were up to. Fiona's passing was part of my life contract of teaching not only through illness but to open a new door regarding physical mediumship. At that moment, I raised my hands in the air and said to Team Spirit, "*I surrender. I have the evidence now that this is possible so I will dedicate myself to this new form of healing work.*"

I contacted David and Jean and we arranged to meet at their place. They had moved from England to Sydney a few years earlier. Their house was in the same area I had lived some years before and I knew in my heart we were meant to cross paths at this time in our lives. The night before I went to their house, I was standing in the kitchen at my house when my flatmate clearly heard drumming coming from my aura. I knew it was physical energy as she was hearing it with her physical senses – it wasn't just me hearing it with my clairaudient psychic sense.

When I arrived at David and Jean's house I immediately felt at home, as though I had known them for many years. David is a highly intelligent man with a successful business background and I could see that his rationality would play an important role in this form of mediumship. Jean, on the other hand, is a much softer personality and radiates beautiful healing energy. They both believe in the power of healing through mediumship and the three of us agreed that this form of mediumship could bring forward great healing, especially for parents who had lost children. We were all excited at the possibilities and knew that it could take many years before the results would come to fruition.

On the first evening with David and Jean, I immediately slipped into a very deep state of consciousness and David and Jean could clearly see light emanating from my aura and faces of people from the spirit world. After a few evenings, a man from the spirit world spoke through me and indicated that they were excited on the other side to attempt to pursue this new form of mediumship with me. They indicated that the road would not be easy and we must all remain patient at the new possibilities that could be brought forward.

Within a month or so, a member of Team Spirit pursuing the physical part of mediumship made himself known to David and Jean. Mayner had now joined the group and for a few hours straight the spirit world answered many questions on life after death from their perspective. The sessions were recorded and David's strong personality was now matched by a similar one in the spirit world as the two of them shared questions and philosophies with one another and answered some of the deepest spiritual questions you could possibly ask. Together, the voice speaking through me in spirit and David began to form a very strong relationship. David was the circle leader and responsible for ensuring the medium was looked after and kept calm throughout the deep altered state of consciousness.

The group was then prompted to invite Roy along as part of this rational team. Roy is actively involved in community work and has a keen interest in spiritual development. Physical mediumship requires this rationality to ensure that those in the room are hearing and seeing with their physical senses and not spiritual senses. The spirit world would not want to spend years pursuing a new form of energy to prove to all humanity there is life after death to find that those in the room were experiencing it at a spiritual level and not a physical level.

Another member, Eddie, was invited to the physical group as he works as a medical scientist and is quite rational about many things in life. I first met Eddie after reading for him in an audience one evening when his wife, Sue, came through with an immense amount of evidence. Through this evidence and confidence in the spirit world, Team Spirit then invited Eddie to come and join the physical group. Through the recent loss of his wife, something positive had emerged and her passing would now bring about greater healing to those in need. Eddie's friend Yolanta was also asked to join and the physical group expanded further. Yolanta has extensive experience in the medical field.

The purpose of physical mediumship is threefold. It is to provide proof to the rational part of the population that there is life after death. This proof would then make the wider population think about their current actions in life and the consequences of those actions through the universal laws of cause and effect, or karma. Once they became aware that every action has a reaction, humans may start to treat one another with more compassion and love and this would evolve the human race on a much higher level.

The second reason is to provide healing to those who are grieving for their loved ones in the spirit world. To hear the voice of their loved ones, see a projection or even feel the energy of their hands on their face would provide immense amounts of healing, especially for parents who have lost children. This is what keeps me patient throughout the whole process and it is this that keeps me focused on attempting to bridge the two worlds together as one.

The third reason for physical mediumship is to bring forward the wisdom and knowledge of those in the spirit world to teach humanity on many levels. At the moment, this information is coming through my physical body through my own vocal cords in a trance state and eventually there may be enough energy for this to be projected outside my physical body and into its own energy field. Either way, these hours of recordings of wisdom will one day be shared with humanity on a much deeper level. But for now, we must be patient with the mechanics of this mediumship to ensure it is finely tuned.

Many people ask if they can be part of the physical group or even sit and observe its work. The spirit world determine who is part of the group and given that it's in the very early stages of development, no-one is allowed to come into the room except for those chosen to sit in the group. The reason for this is that the energy in the room needs to be adjusted by the spirit world for the medium and all the other parties in the room. A slight change in this energy field would distort the ability for them to communicate from the other side. Over the years this will change but for now all information is recorded and kept for future reference.

For this last part of the book, Team Spirit have brought forward some of their own knowledge and wisdom they wish to share with you. I trust in them deeply and I hope you can also close this book with a greater level of understanding and compassion for yourself and other human beings:

From the spirit world, we welcome you into our hearts and minds and know that each and every one of you feels the presence of us throughout your earthly lives. There is no separation between your world and ours and together we are all growing through one another's experiences on various planes of existence.

Once you move into the world of light, your learning will continue on many levels as you pursue both your own paths and assist others in their journeys as well. Do not measure your lives by what you have achieved or gained in a material sense, feel the importance of those who are a part of your lives and the gifts they have brought forward to you. Acknowledge the gifts of exchange you have given to one another and give thanks for all your existence.

Your loved ones in the spiritual realms are never alone, for humanity does not operate on such a level. We are all connected at a deeper soul level and it is this connection that can never be broken. You have all survived many cycles of life and will continue to do so in the future. Much of what you see in the physical world is an illusion that has been placed in front of you to truly attempt to recognise who you are. Never allow anyone to tell you that you are nothing, for you are all loved and treasured by many souls.

World peace is very much dependent upon your everyday thoughts and actions towards one another. Every thought is projected within the realms of existence and no thought is ever lost through translation of intention. If you all intend to have a plane of existence based on peace, then start changing your thoughts towards one another and together the earth will manifest into a more peaceful place.

Never confine who you are based on your physical appearance or mental thoughts of yourselves. These are merely aspects of you based on limitations placed here on earth. You are all living spirit regardless of whether or not you have a physical body. This living spirit can never die and only knows the possibility of continuing to grow and evolve through greater experiences in various worlds of existence.

Do not make your way over to the spirit world with regrets that you did not live life to the full. Do not review your life with a wish that you could have loved more, given more and experienced more. Ask yourself the question that if you were to make your way over to the spirit world today, what would you have changed in your life? From this reflection, start to change your thoughts today and ignite your spirit to be true to itself and live the life that each and every one of you truly deserve.

Louise's next book: *Team Spirit Speaks* will be available by the end of 2011. This book will provide 100 channelled inspirational messages from the spirit world.

www.ingramcontent.com/pod-product-compliance
Lightning Source LLC
Chambersburg PA
CBHW071328190426
43193CB00041B/1010